Alive After the Fall

Alexander Cain

CONTENTS

INTRODUCTION

We live in a world where technology is crucial for our survival. Most of our everyday activities, from flipping a switch to make the lights come on to obtaining our food, all depend on the technology that has developed over the years. Advanced technology has helped us to establish invisible infrastructures that make our lifestyle easier and more comfortable. But, what we fail to consider is how we will survive when and if all of our electronics are devastated. This could happen due to a nuclear attack that triggers a High Altitude Electromagnetic Pulse, commonly referred to as an EMP. It would have a devastating impact on our environment, family, wellbeing, assets, and even the whole region we live in.

With all the events that are happening in the world, it is no news that this kind of attack could happen. Many people consider that an electromagnetic pulse, or EMP, is the most compelling threat to the world. Our food and water supplies, communications, banking, hospitals, and law enforcement, all depend on the electrical grid. Recently, little attention has been given to the ease of generating EMPs by detonating a nuclear weapon in orbit. Thus bringing our civilization to a cold, dark standstill. Events in the Middle East, Eastern Europe, and China, along with the long battle for control of oil assets, bring us to think that such an event is possible.

This book is about some of the measures that an individual can take, in order to prepare for an electromagnetic pulse attack. It is very important to be prepared in advance. In the case of such an attack there is little time to react. Your plan for survival needs to be ready in advance. Although, much of the information is about protecting personal electronic items, it is very important to remember that the greatest threat that comes from the damage of electronic systems is to your family and your wellbeing. This is why your EMP protection efforts should be focused on protecting yourself from the loss of the technological infrastructures that usually sustain our lives.

.

HEMP THREAT

HEMP stands for high altitude electromagnetic pulse. It occurs in the form of a large burst of nuclear electromagnetic radiation. The blast damages electrical currents in wireless antennas, telephone lines and most other forms of electronics we use on a daily basis. In other words, HEMP is caused by the explosion of a nuclear bomb.

Recent studies show that governments in Asia, Russia and the Middle East possess this type of weapon. Every country that has manifested terrorism against the United States could have this technology.

The detonation of a bomb at a high altitude produces a powerful pulse of large amplitude. This pulse is actually generated by the weapons effect on the Earth's ionosphere.

This blast, also known as EMP, produces rapid changes in electromagnetic fields. They generate a spike in voltage and current inside any electronic device. When a nuclear bomb explodes, it unleashes a deadly electromagnetic pulse (EMP), which almost instantly knocks out much of our electrical grid. The electronic control system in our water, oil, and gas distribution will fail. Other infrastructures such as telecommunications and the transportation grid are also affected.

Effects of an EMP event

As said, an EMP is an intense burst of electromagnetic energy that is caused by a sudden and rapid acceleration of charged particles. This can cause all sort of problems with electronic equipment and sometimes, it can even cause physical damage to buildings, vehicles or power lines. There are three factors that we know to cause EMPs: nuclear explosion (HEMP weapon), lighting bolts or solar storms. A big downward surge in particles in the ionosphere would create huge electrical currents that could burn out all kinds of electrical power grids, transformers and other electrical equipment.

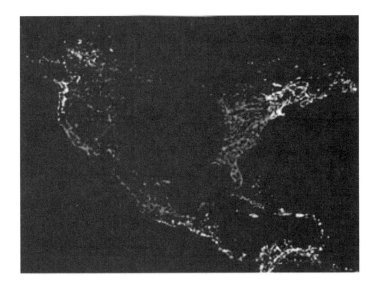

A potential EMP comes either in the form of a manmade nuclear attack or a natural solar flare. Either way, the effects could be disastrous; the devastation would mainly depend on the strength and severity of the pulse and the geographical location. In the worst case scenario, an EMP could result in a total grid- down and loss of every device that runs on electricity, leading the affected region or even an entire continent to resort to primitive measures of survival.

This is why, certain individuals will feel the EMP effects far worse than the others; children, babies, elderly or the disabled will be exposed to a greater risk because these individuals often may require personalized medical care that involves the use of an electronic system.

The consequences of a complete loss of energy will affect our daily activities such as hospitals, businesses, financial transactions, supermarkets and all services and institutions.

Nonetheless, in the case of an EMP, the loss of electricity will not necessarily happen in a town or neighborhood, but it can affect most of the region or even an entire continent. What is worse is that it would probably take up to five years to recover from an EMP.

The first issue that occurs in case of an EMP event is the ability to obtain fuel. Having no electricity leads to a complete shutdown of the refineries and gas pumps. Even if you prepare yourself by stockpiling fuel, gas won't keep more than 6 to 12 months; after that, it degrades so much it becomes muck.

Having no fuel, combined with having no electricity, will automatically lead to a series of traffic problems, as the vehicles will not work anymore. Even if the electromagnetic pulse will not affect all the cars or other vehicles, there will be some that will suddenly stop on the road causing congestion, crashes, and chaos on the roads.

As for electronics, there are high chances that the majority of them will burn out and be destroyed. Unfortunately, scientists do not know the full extent that this damage can cause.

Predicting precise effects of a nuclear EMP is very difficult, depending on the yield of the weapon, the detonation altitude, the geographic latitude, and the magnitude of the local geomagnetic field. In order to protect ourselves from this kind of disaster, it is important to first know the three separate parts of an EMP: E1, E2 and E3. Thus, an EMP produces **three waves of energy**.

The first (**E1**) is a very fast-moving, brief and intense electromagnetic field that can quickly induce high voltage in electrical conductors. It is created when gamma beams from the nuclear explosion knocks electrons out of atoms in the earth's upper atmosphere. These electrons start moving downward and interact with the earth's magnetic field - creating a very large, but short pulse. The E1 component brings most of its damage by making electrical breakdown voltages to be outstripped. In this case, any unprotected micro-hardware will be destroyed; machines and telephones would be over burned by high voltages.

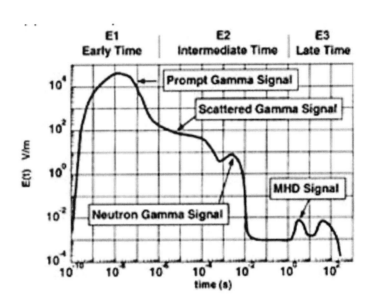

In general, E1 pulses are released by other stars in our galaxy and throughout the whole universe, but the chances of our planet being hit by a pulse like this are very small – there are better chances of Earth being hit by an asteroid, than being hit by E1 pulses from other stars.

The second wave (**E2**) is generated by scattered gamma rays. It is similar to the pulses caused by lightning strikes and tends to be less damaging to the equipment.

The third wave (**E3**) is a much slower pulse, lasting tens to hundreds of seconds, caused by the nuclear detonation driving the earth's magnetic field out in a wave, followed by the field returning to its natural place. It can induce currents in long electrical conductors such as power lines, causing damage to substations and transformers. E3 components will geomagnetically induce currents in long electrical conductors, which can damage or even destroy and burn out electrical equipment such as power line transformers and power grid transformers by inducing huge currents.

The difference between a man-made EMP and a natural one is that a high altitude nuclear explosion or weaponized EMP would most likely contain all these three type of pulses. Where as, a solar storm would only contain the characteristics of an E3 type of pulse. A nuclear EMP would have a very similar effect as a solar storm, when it comes to the E3 pulse, but they also have E1 and E2 pulses.

The proportions of the damage are in direct correlation with the height of the explosion. Thus, a detonation at an altitude of

30 miles will have a damage radius of 480 miles. But at an altitude of 300 miles, the damage would have an effect on a 1470 mile radius.

On the bright side, an EMP attack does not kill people and animals directly, but indirectly it could kill up to 90% of humanity. It doesn't hurt people, but changing electromagnetic fields induce currents in anything capable of carrying current. This is especially true of power lines, where the current can really "build up some steam". But, basically, the electromagnetic pulse could not directly hurt someone physically except in a very specific set of circumstances. For example, it could affect people that have pacemakers or other life sustaining electronic devices in their body, as there is a big chance that EMP could short-circuit them.

The problem with current suddenly showing up where it's not expected is that it can overload circuits. The kind of components and wiring you find in today's electronics can be destroyed by the sort of sudden flow from regular old static electricity.

What is safe from EMP?

Despite the fact that an electromagnetic pulse incident can cause a lot of infrastructure and lifestyle problems, there are some things that can't be affect by an EMP. For example, people, animals and plants are not directly hurt when EMP strikes. The main dangers come from the surroundings.

Despite its power, an EMP does not influence all vehicles. Older models of vehicles with less electrical equipment and more metal in the bodies have a better change of resisting an electromagnetic pulse. The less electrical gadgets they have, the more they will resist at an EMP strike.

EMP – menace and risk

The Earth has experienced EMPs before. The first recorded damage from an EMP came with the solar storm in 1859, otherwise known as the **Carrington Event**. It is considered to be the first and largest documented event of solar flare impacting the Earth. Sunspots and flares could be seen on the sun, followed by a huge geomagnetic storm. The telegraph systems in Europe and North America threw sparks and gave their operators electric shocks.

In 1989, a similar, but milder, storm occurred. It knocked out power supplies in Quebec, jammed radio signals and weather satellites - leading some to believe a nuclear attack was on its way.

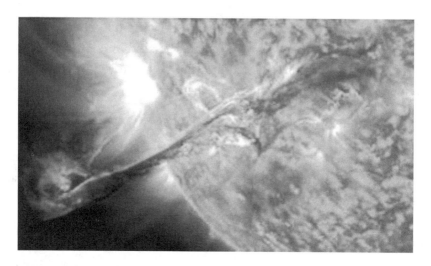

The phenomenon of electromagnetic interference was noticed during the early nuclear tests in the Cold War. British scientists attributed instrumentation failures to what they called 'radio glimmer'.

Direct experience of nuclear EMP effects is limited and not all the data is publicly available. There were a total of about 20 Soviet and US tests, between 1955 and 1962. Many of these were powerful weapons. Its first potential as a weapon was discovered by the US military. In 1962, during the Cold War, the US military detonated a nuclear weapon high above the Pacific Ocean. Known as **Operation Starfish**, this exercise was part of a larger project to evaluate the impact of nuclear explosions in space. In the Starfish Prime test, a 1.44 megaton warhead was launched 900 miles from Hawaii, programmed to explode at 240 miles into space. What was not entirely expected was the amplitude of the resulting electromagnetic pulse (EMP). The pulse knocked out street lights and damaged telephone systems in Hawaii.

A test the same year by Soviet scientists, in Kazakhstan triggered power plant fires. One of the many Soviet **"K-Project"** high-altitudes nuclear experiments appears to have caused the most problems with civilian infrastructure; it caused damage to the overhead power and telecommunication transmission lines, as well as to diesel generators, pulverizing a 350 mile area.

Over the past years there has been a continuous debate over the threat posed by an EMP over modern society. This is one of the nightmares envisioned where in an instant it could destroy the electronic devices and gadgets that civilization has come to depend on. Scientist have tried to simulate what would happen in this scenario, using computers, but the hard data they have is based on the calculations from the last high altitude nuclear EMP from 1962. Also, it is believed that several nations have the ability to produce EMP weapons at least 4 times greater in strength than the tests conducted so far.

The United States set up a commission to assess the threat from an EMP attack, leading to a serious warning that such an event is possible. It concluded that North Korea, Russia, China, India, Pakistan, Iran and Cuba understand how such an attack could happen and that many countries believe the US is able and willing to make an EMP strike in different circumstances. An EMP weapon is far more dangerous and potentially more lethal than a nuclear bomb. It is known that Russia has EMP weapons because of their published research and experiments with various technologies. And now, of course, we can include China. But, actually any nuclear capable nation with an atmospheric delivery system can do this.

The US is drawn to EMP technology and it is potentially non- lethal, but is still highly destructive. An EMP attack would leave buildings standing and spare lives, but it could destroy a sizeable military and infrastructure. Electromagnetic pulses would jam or corrupt important computer data and powerful bursts would completely fry any electronic equipment.

In modern warfare, the various levels of attack could accomplish a number of important combat missions without many casualties. For example an EMP attack could neutralize vehicle control systems, targeting systems or even communication and navigation systems.

PLANNING AND PREPARING

We've established that an EMP incident will fry all electronics whether or not they are plugged in or turned on. This also can damage automobiles, batteries, computers, etc. Life as we know it will change drastically.

Even more concerning is the fact that the strike of EMP is not likely to give any warning.

You don't see or feel it. So, this is the reason why you should be prepared before anything like this can happen.

First of all, the main thing you can do is to ensure your paper documents – keep duplicates of paper records because they are very important. Considering the fact that all electronic devices will stop working without warning, it is recommended to count on paper. This is why you should keep paper records of your finances and possessions, for example, the title to your house and vehicles, marriage authentication, authoritative archives, genealogical records and even photographs of your family and properties.

Planning can be as elaborate as one's time and resources will allow. However, any time and effort spent planning and preparing should be seen as an investment in your future. This planning and preparation is not EMP specific. The basic needs for survival are the same in every scenario: we need food, clean water, shelter and light. With the occurrence of an electromagnetic pulse none of the basic necessities can be taken for granted. Thus, the ultimate preparedness goal should be to provide these necessities without any help from the power grid, generators or fossil fuel.

The Basics

The probability that we will experience an EMP event that will affect the world's power grid is undeniable. Whether the event is as a result of the natural occurring solar flares, or comes at the hands of a nuclear EMP weapon, you have to prepare and cultivate a survivalist mindset. You have to do this in order to keep yourself and your family alive.

Being prepared for an EMP isn't a bad thing, and it doesn't mean that you are hoping one will happen. You are simply thinking about what could happen and taking the necessary steps to ensure that your family is taken care of and that they won't have to do without the very basic necessities.

While we now have some satellites and sensors monitoring solar activity, another event like The Carrington Event could destroy many of the world's largest electrical transformers in power plants and substations across the world. An EMP strike of this magnitude now, would in effect leave as much as half of the earth in complete darkness. Even if we were given some warning before such an event occurred, the power grid would still be affected. However, damage could be kept at a minimum if precautionary blackouts of the electrical grid were done. This could also result in a quicker recovery time although it's difficult to estimate this since a natural EMP strike would potentially affect a larger area than a nuclear EMP strike.

Electrical equipment that can be affected by an EMP:

Equipment for generating electric power - power plants, transformers, solar panels, generators, grid or cable joined batteries.

Communication equipment such as antennas, satellites, radios, cell towers, cell phones, computers, servers can also be vulnerable to an electromagnetic pulse

Transportation. While not all means of transportation can be influenced by an EMP, there are a few innovations that are very vulnerable such as electronic ignition, machines, starter curls or electronic fuel infusion.

Microelectronics can also be very affected by an electromagnetic pulse; basically any silicon chip based engineering.

EMP contains enough energy to destroy anything and everything electronic. Even if cellphones, radios or computers still somehow work, there will be no power grid to charge them. Furthermore, with no power grid, it would be impossible to get gas. Oil refineries need electricity to produce gas, as well as service stations that need electricity to pump gas. Having no gas, it means that there is no way to drive. This means the government cant ship things like food across the country.

Storing food would be a problem too. Without electricity, people can't refrigerate the food. This means that a massive supply of our dairy and meat products would spoil, and be in short supply.

Rebuilding the grid, in the aftermath of EMP events, could take months or even years. Thus, you will need to find ways of become self-sufficient. Having a renewable source of food and water will help you stockpile these items for as long as you need to.

While EMP weapons are usually considered non-lethal, they could easily harm or even kill people if they were directed towards particular targets. For example, if an EMP knocked out a hospital's electricity, any patient on life support would die immediately. Even so in the end, a full-scale EMP attack in a developed country would instantly bring modern life to a more primitive halt.

Protecting your electronic devices

There are a few ways you can protect your electronic equipment. These tips can also protect your devices from lighting strikes, which makes them even more valuable.

First, you should buy quality surge protectors for your main electronics. You can find these for as low as 30 dollars. But keep in mind, that the best surge protectors are UL listed and should comply with UL1449 3rd edition, have a clamping voltage of 330 volts or below, and it have a very fast response time (less than a second).

In order to increase protection, you can add a quality uninterruptible power supply or UPS that is placed behind the surge protector. This method is a little more expensive, costing between $120 (basic models) to over $1000 (improved model).

Homemade protection

Faraday Cages are shielded enclosures made from metallic materials that protect against the effect of an electromagnetic pulse (EMP).

A Faraday cage can protect not only your electronics but an entire chamber or house, from electrostatic discharges produced from an EMP. It can be made of both conductive (aluminum foil) and non-conductive material (cardboard or wood) by directing power and giving regular voltage on all sides of the shielded area.

Faraday enclosures shield their contents from static electric fields. These cages often look distinctly like a cage, but regardless of their appearance, all faraday cages take electrostatic charges, or even certain types of electromagnetic disruptive radiation, and distribute them around the exterior of the enclosure.

By doing that, it cancels out electric charges or radiation within the cage's interior. Simply put, a faraday cage is a hollow conductor, in which the charge remains on the external surface of the cage.

Faraday cages are made from copper mesh and solid aluminum or aluminum foil and a steel trash can, depending on the configuration of the enclosures. This is why you have to consider what and how many devices you trying to protect, before starting building a Faraday cage. This dictates the size of the unit you are creating. For example, E-Steels trashcans are good for a few household electronics, whereas, an entire garage is good for ensuring the functionality of your vehicle in a survival situation and any other items you store there.

How to protect your electronics?

A Faraday cage works by three mechanisms: the conductive layer that reflects incoming fields, the conductor that absorbs incoming energy, and the cage itself that acts to create opposing fields.

One of the most commonly used methods to construct a Faraday cage is by using a steel waste can that has a tight fitting lid on top.

Keep in mind that you have to keep the electronics inside from touching the metal of the can. In order to do that, you have to line the inside of the can with cardboard or any alternate non- conduit.

Otherwise, if you fail to protect the contents within the can, they will wind up centering the EMP exactly towards the gadgets.

To separate your gadgets that you want to keep in your Faraday cage, use a zip-lock static sack. These packs are intended to protect touchy hardware from electrostatic release. Make sure that these packs offer 80 db or more of protection against an EMP event. This is why you would probably have to use more than one layer of static sacks, as none of the items now available are able to give enough protection from an electromagnetic pulse.

After you protected your electronics and lined the can, put the devices in the can and put the lid on. For extra security, you can also secure it with conductive tape so that the top doesn't get detached. Also, remember to look for any holes and crevices between the cover and the can, as it will lose its capacity to protect your gadgets. If you have extra space, try to cover the things in more fabric by using old towels, in order to further protect them from moving and breaking.

Another method to build a faraday cage is by using substantial tinfoil. Make sure that it covers the whole enclosure to create a tight-fitting seal in the same way the lid fits with the waste can.

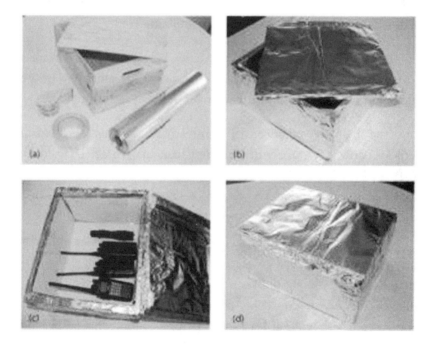

Storing a larger set of electronics might require an entire room for building a Faraday cage. It can be made by lining a room with heavy duty aluminum foil, covering all four walls, the floor, ceiling and the inside of the door.

Moreover, make sure you cover all electrical outlets and light switches with aluminum foil and don't plug anything into the electrical outlets.

In order to prevent the damage of the aluminum foil it is recommended to place a piece of plywood or cardboard on the floor. Rooms built in this way have been shown to offer at least 80db of shielding, but up to several hundred Mhz.

Can a Faraday enclosure have holes?

As long as the holes are significantly smaller comparing to the intensity of the electromagnetic pulse, holes shouldn't be a problem. The problem is that an EMP covers a large recurrence reach, and at some point a gap made by a screw could compromise the whole confinement. This is why it is recommended to use fine conductive mesh when securing an entire room or building.

Taping the seal with conductive tape helps to reduce leakage. Moreover, an elastic gasket or a layer of paint may be very efficient in protecting your gadgets in a Faraday cage.

With the help of engineering, innovative materials and existing methods, nowadays, an entire building can be protected against an EMP strike. Thus, the information and data available make it accessible to us so that we can protect our assets in case of an electromagnetic pulse.

How to protect your building?

The main thing you should keep in mind is that the roof, floors, and walls of all rooms must be covered with a fortified, grounded conductive layer giving at least 80db of protection. This layer can be combined with metal material, conductive paint or any other conductive material.

The conductive layer has to cover the majority of the windows and sun powered panels, where light has to enter.

Remember to disconnect the entire building from the force grid, telephone framework and use only non-conductive water and water pipes.

Another thing you must consider is introducing shielded spinning entryways in order to permit passage. When protecting your building you must equip the enclosure with two sets of entryways that can only be opened at once. Doing this, you don't have to make the structure powerless each time you open an entry. Considering the costs, preparing a building for an electromagnetic pulse with a battery bank and generator, is 30% more than a typical home for new development.

Another good protection for a building is placing little radio wires with ensured circuits that are using surge cover-up with 1 nanosecond clipping times. Keep in mind that the main focus is to have the ability to send good interchanges from inside the building.

What to store in Faraday cages?

The answer is simple: any electronic devices that you find imperative for your survival.

Moreover, you need to consider storing a few things that will provide you and your family with a strategic advantage. Here are some of the most common electronic devices that any individual might need in case of an EMP strike:

- Emergency radio and police scanner
- Flashlights, especially LED electric lamps and lightings
- Rechargeable batteries, charges, battery indicative devices
- Transformers, batteries and wiring and battery meters
- Solar panels, sunlight and wind based charge controllers
- Backup cell phones, extreme SD, Micro SD, USB and other flash memory devices with reinforcements
- Phone systems
- Laptop/PC, calculators (ideally sun oriented) with CD-ROM players and blaze drives
- Network equipment – network routers, modems and switches
- Microwave ovens

- Extra breakers and electronic generator parts
- HAM (Amateur), CB, NOAA, GMRS/FRS, MURS, Marine, Air Band, AM, FM or short radio supplies.
- Spare parts for vehicles
- Night vision and other electronic optics
- Solar battery charges
- Medical Devices – diabetes test meters,   respiratory equipment, blood analyzers, O2 concentrators
- Cordless apparatuses such as drills and saws
- Radiation meters, dosimeters and charges
- Two-way radio

In the aftermath of an EMP attack, be very careful when opening the Faraday Cage. Do not open it immediately after the impact and don't use the electronics, as they will fry in the seconds after the electromagnetic pulse. This is why you should consider having duplicates of the most important and useful items.

You Don't Have to Be Rich to Start Planning

When it comes to an EMP event, there is no discriminating. All levels of income will have the same chances of survival if they take the time to prepare. The best place to start is by making a plan of what you'll need in the event of a crisis and start purchasing items a little at a time. No matter your income level, any small thing you can do to prepare will improve your chances of making it through an EMP attack.

As you begin buying items, start out purchasing those items that are the most important for your survival. These will be items that are necessary to have on hand and are crucial when it comes to your survival. Rather than purchasing these items all at once, you can purchase just a few at a time to build your supply.

Storing food is something that should be near the top of your survival preparation list. Later in this book, you will learn about the different ways to grow, prepare, and store food. Those individuals who already know how to live off the land have an advantage, as they are better able to keep themselves and their families fed.

Being able to grow fruits and vegetables will be a necessary skill if an EMP were to strike. If you don't already know how to do this, you'll want to start growing a small garden beforehand when you aren't relying on this skill for your survival. Gaining the knowledge of what works and what doesn't before it is needed can mean the difference between being self-sufficient and having to rely on someone else's skills to keep you alive in the post-EMP world. Once you are capable of growing your food, you can learn how to can the food as another way to stock up. Canning also works for storing meats and soups for long periods of time.

Water is another item that is essential for survival. When gathering your supplies, you want to gather enough water for everyone in your family. The minimum you should have on hand is one gallon for each person, for each day that it will be needed. Unfortunately, when it comes to an EMP attack, it is anyone's guess to the length of time before the world gets back to normal. That's why we have included different ways to gather and store water later on in this book. Along with the supply of water, you want to make sure you have water purifications tablets, bleach, 2% iodine tincture, and a good water filter on hand.

If anyone in your family takes prescription medication, try to make sure you have a three-month supply on hand.

Pharmacies and doctor's offices won't be able to function after an EMP attack, which means you won't have access to your medications if you run out. If you have access to a mail order pharmacy, take advantage of the fact that they send you three months' worth of your medication at a time.

If you have a baby, making sure you have stocked enough baby supplies. This is not something you want to forget. Every time you purchase diapers, baby wipes and formula, set some aside to build up your stockpile. Add some baby medicine to the list in case they develop a fever or other illness and have extra clothing to keep them warm, especially if you live in a cold area.

While stocking up on toiletries may not be the most important thing for you to consider when preparing for your survival, they can be one of the cheaper items to purchase. Discount shampoo, deodorant, soap, toothpaste, razors, toothbrushes, and toilet paper can all be purchased inexpensively and stored easily.

Planning and prepping for a post-EMP world all at once can end up costing you a lot. That's why it's better to pick up a few items at a time when you go to the grocery store or pharmacy. Smaller purchases made often can add up quickly, without breaking the bank. After awhile, preparing to survive an EMP will become second nature. You will find yourself in the right frame of mind and focused on what you will need to do to survive.

Turn Preparation into a Family Experience

Thinking about a post-EMP world can be a scary thought, especially for the youngest family members. To help them cope with the possibility of an EMP attack and let them know that while things will be different, they'll be okay. Allow the kids to be apart of the preparations. Let them help by picking out some of the supplies. Give them the option to include some of their favorite foods and beverages. Help them see their progress by making a chart where they can check off each food item once it has been collected.

When you go to the store, bring the kids and let them pick out some fun games that don't require electricity. Explain to them that their electronic devices aren't going to work if there is an EMP attack, so they need to pick out some fun things they can do with the family. Allowing the kids to be in charge of the entertainment and spending time doing something together as a family is reassuring for children, even in the event of a disaster.

Another way to assure your children that things will be okay is to talk with them about what people did before there was electricity. Tell them how people lit up their homes, how they prepared and cooked their food, essentially, how they lived life without the convenience of power. Keep things as light and fun as possible when talking to your kids so it won't be so scary in the event an EMP strikes.

Part of your preparedness plan needs to include a meeting place for your family to go to, in case you are not together when an EMP strikes. Sit down together as a family and discuss the best place to meet in case of an EMP strike. Finding your family during the chaos is your number one priority after the disaster to ensure their safety and survival.

Disasters have a tendency to create panic, and pandemonium often ensues shortly after the first wave of the event. The stress and fear will begin to set in as people scramble to figure out how they are going to eat and what they are going to do to survive. It won't take long for chaos to take hold of civilization. You, however, took the time before the EMP attack to prepare, giving you the peace of mind and alleviating the stress.

Preparing well in advance of an EMP has afforded you the ability to feed you and your family and provide them shelter, comfort, and safety. By taking care of the water you will need, you won't have to worry when the water is shut off. You have prepared for when the power grid goes down by ensuring you have a way to provide light and a way to cook the food you have stocked, and you have stocked up on batteries and battery- powered devices.

When the lights do go out, you will have peace of mind because you can provide protection for you and your family. Preparing ahead of time gives you a huge advantage and a better chance of survival. Don't worry what other people think, the only thing that matters is making sure your family is safe and you are prepared for the future.

Your House is Your Shelter

After an EMP attack, your house becomes your most important asset. If you are unable to go anywhere, you will be relying on your home to be your main shelter, which means it is essential that you prepare your home to become self-sufficient and safe. Along with your food and water requirements, there are several other things you need to prepare.

The Perfect Shelter

Before an EMP attack, you'll want to scout a location and find a good source for water. Keep in mind, salt water will need to be purified and desalinated before it can be safely consumed. Therefore, it is best to search for a freshwater source to use.

Next, you will need to make sure that your place of residence has plenty of room for gardening and if you're lucky enough to acquire these, grazing animals. Figuring out what kinds of animals you're going to keep and crops you're going to grow is important as some will require more space than others. Large, full-size livestock breeds will be less manageable than chickens, rabbits, and micro-breeds, and they will also produce less food per acre.

Something else you will need to keep in mind when setting up the perfect shelter is the temperatures of the area where you live. If you live in an area with mild temperatures or one that experiences extreme cold, it is more efficient to create a micro- climate by closing off one room in your home. Trying to heat your entire home with a single wood burning stove, oil lamps, and body heat is not only inefficient, but it is also a waste of the resources that you will have after an EMP attack.

To set up a micro-climate, confine everyone to a single room, saving precious fuels from having to heat the entire house. The room you choose should be well-insulated, in the interior part of your home. Try to avoid a room with windows as they will allow cold air in through the cracks. This is true even with double-paned windows.

During your months of preparation, you need to purchase several rolls of plastic sheeting, staples, and rolls of duct tape.

You will use these to set up your micro-climate. Start by covering the open entrances or doorways, and windows of your chosen room with the plastic sheet. Tape the edges of the sheeting with the duct tape, leaving one edge open to enter and exit the room when needed. Make sure there is proper ventilation around the fireplace and stove and have a battery powered smoke/carbon monoxide detector to keep your family safe from harmful pollutants.

If you plan to use a generator to run an electric stove or other small appliances, do NOT bring it into the room with you. Generators emit carbon monoxide and should be left outside. If you need to, run a large extension cord into the house to utilize the generator.

During times of emergencies, people can become desperate and may try to get to you and your family if they suspect you have a lot of supplies.

They may try to smoke or burn you out, a way to help reduce the risk of losing your shelter from a fire, or being evacuated due to excessive smoke is to find a home made of fireproof materials. If it is within your budget, building a hidden safe room with a second, concealed exit can be a wise investment and keep you and your family safe in any disaster or event.

Building supplies will be a valuable commodity after an EMP attack and should be brought onto your property. Concrete is a good building supply that can protect you from the elements.

When it comes to storing your survival supplies, finding multiple storage facilities for items that can't tolerate variations in temperatures is essential. Items like your food, batteries, and water supplies will need cool, dry storage. Don't keep all of these supplies stored in a single place. Spread the supplies across several areas throughout your shelter, avoiding the easily found and quickly looted "Apocalypse Room."

Easy DIY Projects to Hide Your Goods

In the back of the Linen Closet:

•   Remove the sheet rock at the back of the closet.

•   Build storage shelves between the wall studs.

•   Replace the sheet rock and mount it to the studs with screws instead of nails.

•   Replace the shelves and replace the lining on the shelves to hid the back of the closet.

In the crawl spaces of a finished off attic:

•   Build cubby hole storage areas 6' x 3' tall.

•   Frame both ends of the cubby hole.

•   Install sheet rock with screws to secure it to the frames.

•   Hang a door across the opening that opens outward. Trim this doorway for a final touch.

Having a secure outdoor storage area for equipment, tools, and other necessary items is also an essential part of creating the perfect shelter.

Having a secure outdoor storage area can provide you with a place to hide your valuables and help to slow down looters, causing them to make more noise and use more energy as they try to get to your supplies.

After an EMP attack, there is no telling how people will respond and what people will do to survive. Protecting you and your family from harm should be the first thing on your mind. While gates erected around your home are a good start, you will want to take extra precautions to ensure your home is secure.

The locks that come standard with most doors and fences tend to be flimsy and should be changed out with heavy duty locks that can be found at a local hardware store. Better yet, install double-lock, solid core, steel doors in your home using extra- long lag screws. Before an EMP strike, it is important to take a look around your home and decide on a defensive measure plan. Make sure there is no light coming from the home at night, close off any sound sources that may be heard. It is even important to make sure smells are contained to the inside of your home. This is referred to as enforcing sound and light discipline. In the event the unthinkable happens, you don't want people to know what is inside your home.

Security systems with rechargeable backup batteries and firearms can help protect you and your family. If you haven't been trained in firearm safety, it is important to do so before an EMP emergency. The last thing you want to do is put your safety, and that of your family's at risk because you don't know how to properly use a firearm. Using fire resistant roofing material and adding spark arrestors to wood stoves and fireplace chimneys can prevent your home from burning down. This is important if you find yourself in a wildfire situation or if you are forced to use a food source for your cooking and heating fuel.

When thinking about enforcing sound discipline, one item that will need to be taken care of before a possible attack is an in-home generator. Generators make a lot of noise, and you don't want to draw attention to your living situation, especially when you have amenities that others may be living without. Take the time to build a sound insulated concrete block structure around the generator as a part of your defensive measure plan.

Food and Water

Water is something that you can't live without. While you can survive for weeks without food, you can only go three days without water. Your organs need water to function and survive, without it, they will shut down.

This is one area where it is critical for you to take the time to get it right. Having access to clean water for drinking can mean the difference between your survival and death.

Every day, between 30,000 and 70,000 people die from water-born illnesses, so having access to clean drinking water is essential.

You will also need to have a supply of water for basic tasks like cooking and cleaning. You will also need a supply for basic hygiene that you and your family will need to perform.

While you could go to the store and purchase cases and cases of bottled water, there are alternatives that are easier and cheaper and can last longer if needed. Having an ample water supply can keep you and your family alive for days, weeks, and even months.

Finding Water

Finding water in an **urban setting** can be as simple as using a water catchment system to collect runoff water from roofs. When using this method, using a metal roof is best as it contains fewer chemicals and pollutants than an asphalt shingle roof. Be careful to avoid roofs that are heavily contaminated with bird feces, adhesive chemicals and other contaminants commonly found in roof construction.

When catching rainwater, you want to establish a good flow in order to allow contaminants to be washed from the surface of the roof, rather than into the water you will use for your plants or drinking water.

You can accomplish this by waiting a while for the water to run before you place a barrel or catch container under the flow of water or by installing pipes and valves to divert the water flow for a bit before being routed into your storage tanks.

For this method, 50 gallons or larger, opaque food-grade, plastic containers work best as they can be filled by attaching a small piece of pipe to your rain gutter, and they come with a pre- filter.

Catching rainwater isn't the only source of water for those living in urban areas. Other acceptable sources of water include water bottling companies and their delivery trucks, water coolers, rooftop water tanks, water heaters, swimming pools, rivers, ponds, lakes, or melting snow or ice. Melting ice as opposed to snow will provide you with more water while using same amount of fuel.

If you are in an area that sees an ample amount of snowfall during the year, melting snow can be a great source for your water supply. To melt the snow, take a large stockpot and melt a little bit of snow to start. As the snow begins to melt into water, add more snow to the warm water to utilize the water's greater density and specific heat melt to continue to melt the smaller amounts of snow. This will decrease the amount of time it will take to melt the snow and conserve your fuel.

When you are looking for a water supply, it is important to find the least contaminated source that is available. The first water sources to be depleted will be in the inhabited areas, followed by the commercial areas. Less obvious sources like water heaters and toilet tanks will be the final sources to be depleted.

If you live in a **rural area**, your water sources will be less likely to be contaminated, but it is important to test any source that may be suspect. Test the water ahead of time if you have stored drinking water test kits.

Some things you will need to look out for are fecal contamination, industrial contamination, and contamination from pesticides. Take some time and check upstream for any possible sources of pollution. Do what you can to dissuade others from using the water source for disposing of waste, washing laundry, washing dishes, or bathing to keep soaps and other contaminants out of your water source.

You can find better quality water in dripping springs, flowing springs, wells, artesian wells and fast moving streams. If you have access to a deep well, you will need to make sure to have the manual equipment necessary to draw water without electricity.

This can be hand-pump well heads, manual well buckets, lines, or other manual equipment. It is also a good idea to store alternative energy equipment like battery powered electric pumps and whatever else you will need to keep your well working.

There are some areas where you will be able to dig a well by hand or develop a spring with improvements to obtain your water source. To accomplish this, you will want hand tools, pipes, buckets, and construction materials on hand.

Something to keep in mind: Digging your own well, spring, or dam may affect others downstream. The last thing you want to do is start a feud over water rights.

Storing Water

While you are collecting water, you will need to make sure it is passing through a pre-filter to remove large contaminants. Once this phase has been accomplished, you will need to let the water settle. Let the water sit undisturbed for a period, to allow the heavier particles to settle to the bottom of the container. This further reduces the contamination levels, which allows your filter or water purifier to last longer.

After the water has settled, it is ready to be filtered, disinfected, and purified. A siphon pump is a good investment as it makes it easier to retrieve the water and move it to other containers.

Just like food, untreated tap water needs to be rotated out. The water, when untreated, contains small amounts of bacteria and algae that will grow under the right set of circumstances.

Like your food, it is important to label the dates on your containers of water. Water from the tap will keep for about six months; however, you always want to check the water first to ensure it looks clean. Properly stored water should be rotated once a year.

Properly disinfected tap water can be stored for much longer, up to 30 years or more if it is stored in disinfected, opaque, airtight water barrels without being opened. It is important to use **new, clean, quality water containers** and a contaminant free filling process to ensure your water source is free from contaminants.

Don't use a regular garden hose to fill the containers. Instead, use a drinking water quality hose like those that are used to fill the water tank on an RV. When treating the water for contaminants, use a high-quality additive like chlorine dioxide or a copper/silver ion compound. Resort to using chlorine bleach only in the event of an emergency.

Keep in mind:

- Don't use second-hand containers for water storage.
- Use containers that are air-tight and have an air-tight seal.
- Label the containers as "drinking water" and be sure to include the storage date.
- Keep the water stored at a constant, cool temperature.
- Keep away from toxic substances like pesticides and fuel.
- Keep the water out of direct sunlight.
- Don't store the containers directly on concrete to avoid radon contamination.

Disinfecting and Purifying

The water that you gather for your supply will need to be disinfected and purified before you can use it.

If the water barrels that you are using are non-UV treated, you will have to monitor the integrity of the barrels as they can break down by UV light sources over time. The water you collect can become contaminated by bacteria, algae, and other contaminants every time you open the barrel. You can make contaminated water drinkable through water filtration, purification, and distillation processes.

According to the EPA, a **water filter** must have the ability of 4 log contamination reduction, in other words, it must be able to remove 99.99% of the contaminants. A **water purifier** must have the ability of 6 log contamination reduction, or it must be able to remove 99.9999% of all contaminants, leaving no more than 1 part per 10 million. What does this mean for you? If you have water that is suspect, you should run your water through a water filter. If your water supply might have highly dangerous contaminants, you should use a water purifier to disinfect and purify the water.

The first step in the water filtration process is pre-filtration. By pre-filtering the water, you will extend the life of your water filters. For a cost-effective pre-filter, use a coffee filter that you can pick up at any grocery store. To use, simply place the filter in a container and pour the water in, allowing the large particulates to be strained out of your drinking water.

Another option for filtering suspect water is something called a water filter straw. This allows you to drink straight from a stream, spring, or other water sources. As the water passes through the layers of the straw, it is filtered, providing you with water that is as clean as the water you get from the tap. The straws are lightweight and are easy to carry. They can also be set up as gravity filters, which will allow you to filter large quantities of water at a time to store for future use.

Investing in a water test kit is a wise decision. Test kits are used to measure harmful levels of bacteria, pesticides, lead, and other dissolved solids. They can be used to make sure your purifying system is working. Using a test kit on your water before consuming it will help keep your family from becoming sick due to drinking unsafe water.

Unscented chlorine bleach contains free chlorine, which loses its potency over time, usually between six months to a year. With this in mind, you may want to put together an emergency bleach making kit. Instructions on how to put together an emergency bleach making kit can be found online.

When putting together your emergency bleach making kit, it is best to use food grade calcium or sodium hypochlorite with 60% - 70% free chlorine, if it is available. These items can be stored for up to ten years before their potency begins to diminish. For between $15 and $40, a single bleach making kit has the potential to disinfect drinking water for your entire neighborhood for several years.

Along with your drinking water, you will also need to have a supply of water for your crops and animals, as well as for maintaining proper hygiene and cleaning. If you have a swimming pool, this can be a great water storage container for this kind of water as it can hold thousands of gallons of water. You can purchase a filtration or purification system to purify the water in the pool or water from a river or creek.

Along with the various types of filtration and purification devices that you can purchase, there is also a variety of chemical disinfectant tablets, powders, and drops that are on the market to disinfect water. The most common of these is chlorine dioxide and iodine.

When using these types of chemical disinfectant products, follow the directions according to water turbidity level and temperature. You will have to use more of the chemical for colder, cloudier water, and the water will need to sit longer for the disinfectant to do its job.

Did you know?

Along with killing harmful micro-organisms found in contaminated water sources, a 2% tincture of iodine can be used for first aid.

If your water is clear and temperate use five drops of iodine per quart of water and allows it to sit for half and hour. If your water is cloudier and has a lower temperature, you will need to use up to 10 drops of iodine, and it will have to sit longer, upwards of two to three hours. To decrease the cloudiness of the water, pre-filter it and allow the water to settle.

To increase the temperature of the water and preserve your iodine supply, place the water in a dark container and let it sit in direct sunlight, or simply heat the water. Not only will this preserve your iodine supply, but it will also help to improve the taste of the water.

Until the disinfection process is completed, avoid adding powdered drink mixes to the water. Once the process is complete, adding flavored mixes can mask the chemical flavor and replace electrolytes and salts if you have become dehydrated.

Another way to disinfect water is with 6% unscented chlorine bleach. Just 3 to 5 drops per quart will have the same effects as the 2% iodine tincture.

Although time-consuming, boiling your water is another safe way to disinfect it before drinking. A potential downfall to boiling is that it uses a lot of fuel, which can become problematic. The water needs to reach a rolling boil to kill any harmful micro-organisms in the water, including Cryptosporidium Parvum and Giardia. Remember, it's what you can't see in the water that will make you sick or even kill you.

If you are faced with an emergency, you can improvise you own layered filter system using charcoal, activated carbon, sheets, coffee filters, baked sand, kerchiefs, or other filtration materials available to you. If you have to use one of these methods, and you have fuel available, be sure to boil the water to kill anything that your improvised filter system may have missed.

Easy Charcoal Water Filter Items needed for the project:

- 2-liter soda bottle
- Sand
- Charcoal
- Scissors or sharp knife for cutting the bottle
- A piece of cloth
- A second, larger container

First you will need to cut off the end of a 2-liter soda bottle. Place a piece of fabric in the smaller opening to prevent the charcoal from falling out. Crush the charcoal and place it in the container, creating a matrix for the water. You can add a second piece of cloth, sand or grass on top of the charcoal. Place the soda bottle with the charcoal on top of the second container and slowly pour in the untreated water. Clean water will slowly drip out of the bottom of the filter and into the second container.

If you only have salt water available, it is possible to turn it into fresh water. Take a fairly large pot and place an empty glass cup, preferably Pyrex glass or metal in the center of the pot. Slowly pour some salt water into the pot. Don't overfill the pot, stopping well below the mouth of the glass.

Place the pot lid upside down so the highest point, or handle is facing down, directly above the glass. Next, bring the water to a slow boil. The vapor from the boiling water will begin to condense on the surface of the lid and run down to the lowest point (the handle) and drip into the glass.

The salt from the water will remain at the bottom of the large pot. The process is slow going, it will probably take 20 minutes or more to complete and will use a substantial amount of fuel, but it could be what helps you survive. The water and the glass will be extremely hot so you have to wait for them to cool down before you can drink the water.

Creating a Filter Using:

Apple and Tomato Peels

Peel some apples and tomatoes and place the peels in a rubbing alcohol solution. Let them soak for 20 minutes before removing. After removing, place them on a clean surface and allow them to dry out.

Once they peels are completely dry, place them in a container with the water that needs to be purified. You will need to wait a few hours before drinking the water.

Sunlight

Take some plastic water bottles and fill them with water. Place them in the sunlight for at least six hours. The sun's ultraviolet rays' will kill any parasites in the water. For this method to work, the water has to reach 30 degrees Celsius, or 86 degrees Fahrenheit for a minimum of five hours.

Citrus Juice

To clean up water for drinking purposes, put a squeeze of citrus juice in the water. To speed up the process, place the water in sunlight. For the best results, use the juice from a lime.

Storing Food

Storing food is a very efficient method in order to avoid going hungry when the food supply in stores runs out; this is highly likely to happen in the event of an EMP incident.

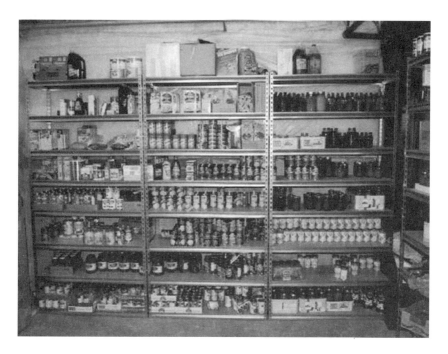

When starting to accumulate food, remember that your pantry and freezer store counts. Create and maintain a full stock of supplies by purchasing a few extra items you would usually purchase each time you go shopping, until you reach the level you feel necessary. Then rotate your stock by eating from your supplies and continually replacing with new purchases.

Stockpiling food is not necessarily a luxury. You can use discount coupons to buy non-perishable food that is on sale. Why choose non-perishable food? Because with the electricity going down your freezer or other cooling devices will definitely not work anymore, so you will need long-term food that meets your nutritional needs and are high in proteins and vitamins. It is estimated that a year worth of provisions for one person can total up to **around $800.**

Best foods to stockpile

Dried foods. Drying or dehydration is an excellent way to preserve food. Properly dehydrated foods do not require refrigeration. They can be stored in airtight containers or plastic bags and will keep for a year or even longer. Dehydrated vegetables are great to use in soups and stews and many dehydrated fruits are delicious without rehydrating them.

Dried goods that you might consider storing include dried beans, corn, coffee beans and other grains. Brown rice is a very good source of vitamins and minerals and is very easy to prepare.

Canned foods. Canning implies the complete sterilization of the food, eliminating all traces of microbes. Properly canned food will last almost indefinitely, but they quality will begin to deteriorate after a year maybe two. This is by far the best option when it comes to food storage because it doesn't need to be refrigerated and requires minimal to no preparation before serving. Canned foods are a good option because they also contain a fair amount of water.

Raw nuts – unsalted and unroasted nuts are great. They are an excellent food source as they have proteins, fatty acids, vitamins and minerals. There are many types of nuts you can chose from such as sunflower seeds, peanuts, almonds, chestnuts, walnuts and many others.

Beans – dried or canned, can last around 8 to 10 years. You can choose from a different range of beans such as: pinto beans, kidney beans, lima beans, lentils, adzuki beans and many others.

Hard grains – properly stored, hard gains have a shelf life up to 12 years.

Spices - are a great way to add a little flavor to the foods you are stockpiling. Salt, sugar, pepper, honey and even alcohol can be stored for over 10 years, if they are stored in a moisture free container. Also, stockpiling onions and garlic is a very good idea because these root vegetables are natural antihistamines and will help you prevent possible illnesses.

Flours – hermetically sealed, flours can last up to 5 years at a stable temperature of 70 degrees F. You can consider storing unbleached flour, white and whole wheat flour or cornmeal.

Pasta – if kept dry, they can store longer than flour. Types of pastas you should consider storing are noodles, spaghetti, macaroni, and ribbons.

You can even stockpile chocolate, energy bars, powdered milk, candies and soda. These are excellent providers of energy. Even though, you may have complete food storage, in case of a disaster there will be times when you will have to adapt to what Mother Nature has to offer. As we all know, there are a lot of wild plants in nature that are recommended to consume. Here are some of the most common **edible plants**:

Blackberries   Dandelions   Pigweed

Chicory leaves   Elderberries   Mullberries

Keep in mind that not all plants are edible! Below you can find a list of some of the most common **toxic plants** that you should definitely avoid:

Plants and herbs are not only the only resource of food, in times of need. In the aftermath of an EMP, if your stockpiling food preparations have failed and you remain out of resources, **fishing** is a great method you can procure food, especially meat which is essential in a survival diet.

White snake root   Angel's trumpets   Rosary Pea

Water Hemlock   Rhubarb   Daphne

Keep in mind that fishing is only possible in waters that are safe and unpolluted, as there are big chances of ecological disasters, when an EMP strikes.

Despite the fact that fishing is considered to be a great way of getting off the pressure, it is the safest activity you can do to acquire food. It does not require many resources, you just need a river or lake, fishing rod, bate and a lot of patience.

How to make your own fishing rod from resource you have at your hand.

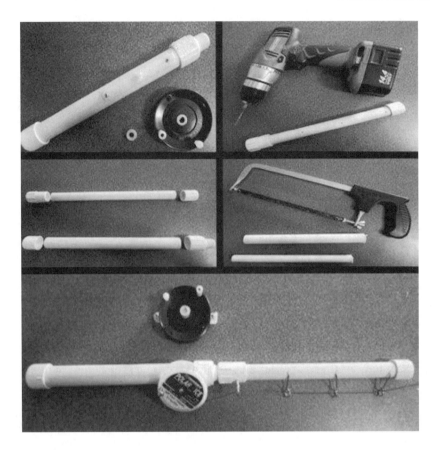

Using PVC pipes

- •   Two PVC pipes
- •   Two end caps
- •   Hacksaw
- •   Sandpaper
- •   Electric tape
- •   Fishing line
- •   Hooks and sinkers

1.   Cut two PVC pipes, one a half an inch in diameter and the other ¾ of an inch. The pipes can be as long as you need, keeping in mind that the combined length of the pipes will be the length of all the fishing rod.

2.   Smooth the fresh cut edges of the pipes and remove any marking from their body.

3.   Take one of the end caps and make a hole in it. Make sure you clean the cap after you made the hole, so the lanyard doesn't get caught on rough edges. Take the cordage and put the ends through the hole so the knot is inside the end cap. After tying the knot, make sure that the loop is big enough.

4.   Add the fishing line on the pipes and put electric tape on the knot so that the line doesn't get caught while casting.

5.   Now it's time to add the steel liter, hooks and sinkers. Tie the steel liter to the line.

Using a wooden stick

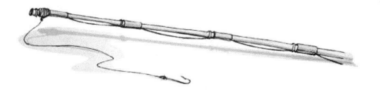

1.   Find a suitable long wooden stick. Its length can be between 8 and 10 feet long with 1 or 2 inches diameter.

2.   Trim away leaves or nubs and smooth the cane, using a sharp knife. For smoothing, you can use sandpaper.

3.   After, test the stick with a few swings, to make sure it doesn't break or bend. The fishing cane has to be as straight as possible.

4.   Attach the fishing line. Use Dacron line and tie one end, leaving a couple of inches for the handle. Run the line along the cane

until you get to the end. Then, use extra fishing line and tie the running line to the fishing pole at two different points. The length of the fishing line should measure the total length of the stick, plus an extra two feet.

5.   Finally, attach the hook, bobber and sinker to the end of the line.

Cooking your food and heating water

Cooking your food and heating your water is another problem you have to face when it comes to survival. With no electricity for refrigerators meat, poultry, fish, and dairy become perishable foods that require careful preparation in order to avoid any food poisoning.

There are a few ways to prepare your food, such as: a wood stove or oven made of tin cans, charcoal grills, candles, the sun or outdoor campfires.

A wood stove is an efficient way that helps you prepare your food, because it can reduce the quantity of wood you're using by one third.

Additionally, if you're using an indoor stove, the ventilating pipes cleanse the air. Using the right fuel will help you save money and produce heat properly, this is why the wood should be stored for drying for at least 6 months.

To keep it dry, you simply have to cover it with an impermeable cover such as a plastic sheet. You don't have to build large fires; a small fire is the best choice.

When starting the fire, add small pieces of wood and then add larger pieces one at the time to maintain it (don't throw all large pieces in at once). Also, it is recommended to keep the stove door open for about one minute so that the fire can burn strongly, but remember that you have to keep them closed most of the time to prevent losing heat.

Charcoal grills are another viable option for outdoor cooking. Charcoal is a cheap fuel and is widely available, but what is important to remember is that you can prevent wasting this fuel by using small grills with tightly closed vents.

Keep in mind that charcoal has to be stored in dry places in order to prevent moisture damage. You can buy charcoal grills at camping stores or you can find them even on the internet. Also, if you don't have one it is very easy to build a charcoal grill using only tin cans: use a punched tin can, place paper at the bottom of it, set it on fire and then place the charcoals above.

Using candles is another option you can try, but this method is more useful for boiling water rather than cooking.

The more candles you're using, the faster the water boils. This is why you should consider having candles in your stock supply when making preparations.

Solar cooking is the simplest, safest and most convenient way to cook food without consuming fuels. Basically, the sun is the ultimate renewable energy source, thus sunlight is the only fuel needed. The golden rule of solar cooking is to get your food early in the day.

A solar cooker needs an outdoor spot that is sunny for several hours and is protected from wind or rain. This is why solar cookers don't work at night or in cloudy conditions, so preparing your food in a solar cooker depends very much on timing and weather. As we know, dark surfaces get very hot in sunlight, so it's recommended to cook food best in shallow dark thin metal pots with dark lids to hold in heat and moisture.

Solar cookers or ovens are increasingly used to reduce reliance on firewood and other fuels. It can be an effective energy-saving addition to your cooking methods.

Make your own solar cooker:

• Cardboard box

• Tape

• Aluminum foil

Cut the cardboard box in half, using scissors or knife, in two large rectangular pieces.

Each piece is composed of one square face of the box together with one flap.

Then, draw all the fold lines at 15 ° angles, cut the lines and fold along the folded lines.

Glue the aluminum foil onto the inner side of the rectangular pieces.

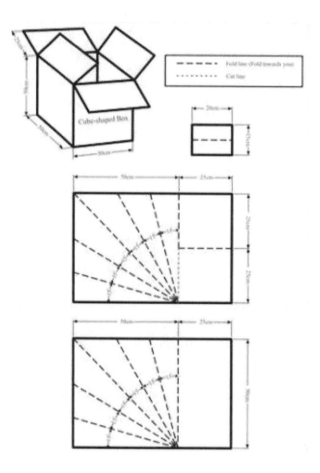

Join the two large rectangular cardboard pieces together with tape just like the image below:

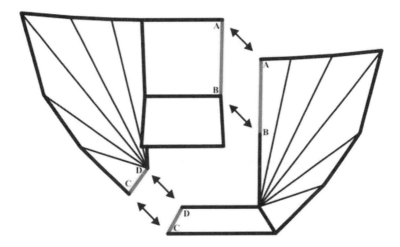

To finish your solar cooker, all you have to do is glue the outer sides of the left cardboard's bottom and place it on top of the square basis of the right cardboard.

It should look like this:

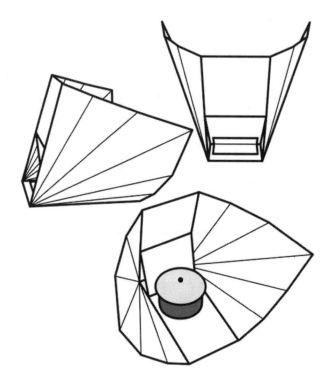

First Aid

Medicine

In the aftermath of an EMP attack, having enough medical supplies is going to be essential. While you are preparing your house, gather supplies from your pharmacy during every visit, or grab medical supplies when you do your grocery shopping.

You will need to have needles, suture kits, aspirin, over-the-counter medications, ointments, and other medical supplies on hand in case of an EMP attack. Any medical item that you might use in your everyday life as it is now will probably be needed after an EMP as well.

- Cranberry juice
- Cloves

These are only a few items that you can use as alternative medicines. There are plenty of books that provide in-depth information on the best plants and herbs to use and what they can treat. Later in this section we will discuss these alternative medicines in a bit more detail.

Storage of Heat Sensitive Medicines

If you have medication that you need to store at a certain temperature, it is recommended you invest in a Pot-in-a-Pot Refrigerator.

Making a Pot-in-a-Pot Refrigerator

A simple pot-in-a-pot refrigerator can be improvised by using a smaller clay pot within a larger clay pot. Add sand and water in between the smaller and larger pot. Cover the top of the small pot with a rag so the inside of the smaller pot will become cool, allowing you to store heat sensitive medicines. The only maintenance that this device needs is water to be added to the sand on a continuous basis to keep the inside of the small pot cool.

Antibiotics

Before you find yourself in a post-EMP world, learn how to store antibiotics properly. There is a handful of antibiotics you will want to keep on hand to keep your family healthy. Antibiotics like Amoxicillin, Flagyl, Cipro, Ampicillin, Keflex, and Doxycycline are all important antibiotics that you will want to have on hand and readily available.

If you haven't received training in first aid, you should take a class with the Red Cross. Your local YMCA may offer classes, or they can be taken from private businesses in your community. During these classes, you will gain valuable skills such as CPR, first aid, and disease management.

You will also learn how to identify and treat three of the most common killers in an emergency: obstructed airways, excessive blood loss, and shock.

Alternative medicines such as medicinal seeds and healing herbs can take care of certain medical conditions should the need arise. Have books on hand to refer to in case you are not sure of what to do. Here are a few items you may want to have on hand to use as alternative medicines:

- Garlic tea
- Cinnamon
- Eucalyptus
- Iodine meat tenderizer
- Cayenne pepper

All of these antibiotics are ones that can only be prescribed by your doctor and you are always given the instruction that you must "finish all of the medication." So how can you possibly store as much of these antibiotics for an upcoming disaster? There are plenty of doctors who advertise on-line that they are willing to provide extra prescriptions for these types of non-controlled medications specifically for the purpose of emergency preparedness.

Many of the medicines that we are prescribed are the same ones that are given to animals. They come off the same production lines at the manufacturers. You can purchase the same antibiotic your doctor prescribes right off the shelf of your local veterinarian's office, and you don't need a prescription to purchase these medications.

Doxycycline is labeled as "bird biotic," while Amoxicillin can be found under the name "fish-mox forte." Many of the bottles are clearly labeled as Amoxicillin, making it easy for you to spot.

Take the time to do and Internet search for the description of the medication through a pill identification site to make sure that the medication is also safe for human consumption.

If you've been under the impression that your unused medication that has passed its "use by" date is no longer effective, you, like so many others, have been lead astray. All manufacturers of medicines are required to put a date on their medications; however, very few of them lose their effectiveness after this date. Take the time to research all of your medications carefully, since a few of them, like the wide-spectrum antibiotic tetracycline become toxic after expiration.

The US military has conducted some studies on the effectiveness of expired medication. They found, with very few exceptions, the majority of medications retain their therapeutic value, decades after the expiration dates printed on the labels. However, they warn you need to be diligent in your research to be positive about the medications you are taking.

The key to getting the most out of your antibiotics is to keep them properly stored in a cool environment out of direct sunlight. Heat can render an antibiotic useless, so don't leave the medication in a room that is constantly hot. A good way to store them pre-EMP is to vacuum-seal them and place them in the freezer. This will keep them from breaking down.

First Aid Kit

In any case of disaster, weather is an EMP attack or even a natural incident, the main concern should the security and health of you and your family. As we know by now, following an EMP all the communication systems will be down, so going to the hospital or calling for emergency services will be an impossible task. With the electricity going down local services and officials cannot reach everyone affected. Even if these services are trying their best. A disaster supplies kit is simply a collection of basic items your household may need in the event of an emergency. Try to assemble your kit very well in advance.

You will need to survive on your own after an EMP strike; this means having your crucial supplies for a pretty long period of time.

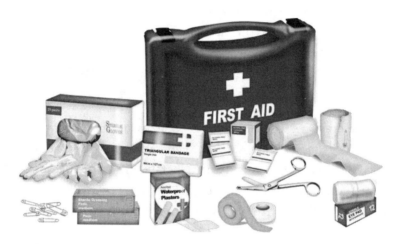

A well-stocked first aid kit can help you respond immediately to common emergencies or injuries. You should consider having one or even more supply kits: keep at least one first aid kit in your home and one in your car or office. Store them in easy to retrieve locations.

The last thing you want to be doing during a medical emergency is familiarizing yourself with your first aid kit. The pre-packaged first aid kits you can purchase at the store are put together based on the idea that you will be using it under normal living conditions. If you do purchase a pre-packaged kit from the store, be sure to pick one that says "survival first aid kit" on the outside.

If you can't find a pre-packed kit made specifically for long-term survival, then you will want to put one together yourself that includes everything you will need to survive after an EMP attack or other disasters. The first thing you will need to purchase is a sturdy bag to store the supplies.

First aid kits are not intended for long-term treatment. If you have a single serious injury, it could quickly deplete your first aid supplies. To survive after an EMP attack, you need to start thinking in terms of weeks and months, not days. It is quite possible you will be changing bandages and applying ointments long term.

When dealing with possible injuries, you want to have first aid training, as well as having first aid manuals on hand. You can also pick up one-page laminated sheets that list all types of injuries that you might face. If you are the only one in your group with first aid training, the manuals and a laminated sheets can assist someone else in the chance you are the one who has been injured.

Here is a list of supplies you will want to put in your first aid kit:

Basic supplies

- Adhesive bandages and cloth tape in assorted sizes
- Roller bandages in assorted sizes
- Triangular bandages
- Cotton swabs and pads
- Gauze pads
- Latex or synthetic gloves
- Antibiotic ointment packets
- Antiseptic solution and wipe packets
- Saline solution
- Soap or hand sanitizer
- Thermometer
- Adhesive tape
- Duct tape
- Plastic bags
- Scissors, tweezers and safety pins
- First aid manual

Emergency supplies

- Important paperwork and insurance documents
- Hand crank flashlights and radios
- Candles and matches
- Emergency space blanket
- Sunscreen
- Multi-purpose knife\tool
- Dust masks
- Needle and thread
- Area maps
- Sleeping bags

Medicines

- Aspirin and pain relievers
- Breathing barrier
- Activated charcoal
- Aloe Vera gel
- Alcohol
- Antihistamines for allergies
- Calamine lotion
- Personal medication
- Syringe and medicine cup or spoon

In any case, if your medicine supplies run out you might have to improvise and rely on what nature has to offer or what other resources you have at your hand. It is very important to know what to stockpile when preparing for emergency cases. Here are some of the most important and common natural medicines you should stockpile:

Ginger can be used not only as medicine but as a spice, too. It can be used fresh, dried, powdered or as juice or oil. Ginger is very useful to treat various types of stomach problems, nausea, pain relief, muscles soreness and many respiratory infections that can lead to cough and bronchitis.

Cinnamon reduces the blood sugar levels; therefore it is very popular with people with diabetes that take it to control their blood sugar variations. Also, it has been found that cinnamon is an effective natural remedy for eliminating headaches and migraine relief.

Peppermint is one of the nature's most valuable herbal remedies. Its therapeutic effects have been known since ancient times and it is used for the common cold, cough and inflammation of throat, sinus infections and respiratory infections.

Also, it is very useful for digestive problems including heartburn, nausea, vomiting and many gastrointestinal problems.

Cayenne pepper is useful for a variety of ailments such as heartburn, tremors, fever, and sore throat. It is a very good anti cold and flu agent and also it can prevent the formation of the fungal pathogens. Moreover, cayenne pepper is an efficient pain reliever; just rub the area affected but remember not to use it in open wounds.

Chicory root has a long history of providing support to liver problems. It can also provide support for digestive problems such as constipation and it is considered to be a rich source of antioxidants.

Basil is not only a very efficient antibiotic and antibacterial agent, but interestingly, it can be used as a bug repellent, too.

Iodine tincture is not only good for cleansing the water, but it is a very useful antiseptic; it is a wonderful wound cleaner. Moreover, iodine is a powerful antioxidant.

Baking soda can be used for treating insect bites and itchy skin. Make a paste out of baking soda and water, and apply it onto affected skin. It can also be replaced with some of personal care products such as toothpaste or deodorant. Baking soda is known for neutralizing odors.

How to give first aid?

After an EMP strike, all communication systems will be down, thus going to the hospitals or even calling for ambulance is not a viable option.

So, in order to be fully prepared, it is recommended to take first aid courses and learn how to correctly perform CPR.

Basic first aid means to asses and address the needs of someone who has been injured or is in physiological distress due to a heart attack, choking, allergic reactions or other medical emergencies.

It allows you to quickly determine a person's physical conditions and the correct course of treatment

Learning how to perform cardio-pulmonary resuscitation, or CPR, saves lives. Basic CPR consists of chest compression and rescue breathing.

Everyone in your family or group should take one of these courses and should have the CPR skills tested at least every two years.

CPR is typically administered in cases of cardiac arrest. Signs of cardiac arrest include an absence of heartbeats, blood flow and pulse. When blood stops flowing to the brain, the victim becomes unconscious and stops regular breathing.

Remember that the rules of CPR are airway, breathing and circulation; these will help you perform the correct cardio- pulmonary resuscitation.

The first thing you should consider when performing CPR is the **airway**. If the person has collapsed and lying flat on his or her back, roll him or her over moving the entire body at one time.

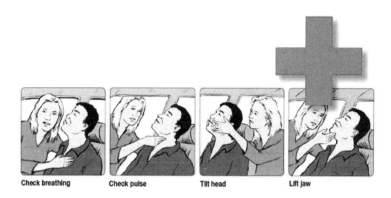

Check breathing   Check pulse   Tilt head   Lift jaw

Once the airways are open, check to see if the person is breathing. Take 5 to 10 seconds to verify normal **breathing**. Pinch the person's nose shut and keep your hand on the person's forehead to maintain the head tilt.

Once you do that, inhale normally before giving **rescue breath** to victim. Immediately give two full breaths while maintaining air-tight seal with your mouth on the victim's mouth. Each breath should be one second in duration and should make the victim's chest rise. Avoid giving too many breaths or breaths that are large and forceful.

After giving two full breaths, immediately begin **chest compressions**. With one hand, locate the notch where the bottom rims of the rib cage meet in the middle of the chest. Place the other hand on top and press downward, keeping your arms straight by pushing hard and fast.

Then, relax the pressure completely. Relaxation and compression should be of equal duration. Use 30 chest compressions to every two breaths. It is recommended to compress at the rate of about 100 times per minute.

In case of choking, it is very important to know the Heimlich maneuver by performing abdominal thrusts.

Stand behind the person that is in distress, circle your arms around the abdomen and tip the person forward slightly.

Make a fist with your dominant hand and place it slightly above the person's navel and under the breastbone.

Wrap the fist with the other hand and press hard into the abdomen with quick upward thrusts, using good force as if trying to lift up the person.

If needed, perform a total of 5 abdominal thrusts and if the blockage still isn't dislodged, repeat the cycle.

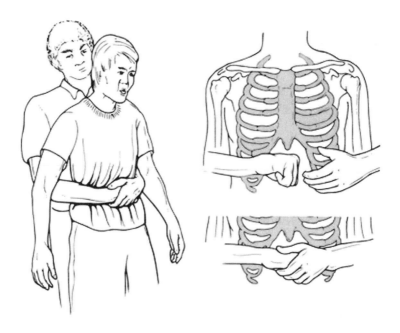

Other Basic Necessities

Despite all the preparations you are making in case of EMP strike, you don't forget about toiletries. Even though, now they may seem like a luxury, in a survival situation they become a real necessity.

As the main concern is keeping you and your family clean and healthy, sanitizing your entire house will diminish the risk of developing allergies or other serious conditions like dysentery, tetanus, cholera or typhus. This is very useful in survival situations, when going to the drug store or procuring medication seems like an impossible mission. Thus, when prepping for a disaster you should always consider about basic necessity items.

Here is a checklist of toiletries that you might need:

- Cleansers
- Antiperspirant
- Razors
- Tissues
- Toothpaste, toothbrushes and mouth wash
- Soaps
- Disinfectant
- Children/baby care items
- Needle and thread

Tools

After an EMP attack, your power tools will be useless unless they are battery operated and can be recharged with a solar charger or a generator and fuel. Hand tools, though harder to use, never require electricity.

There are some basic tools that you will want to have on hand. This includes hammers, screwdrivers - both flat head and Philips' head - wrenches, pliers, vice grips, tape measure, saws, levels, utility knives, and a supply of hardware and fasteners. Home improvement stores carry a variety of tool kits containing these tools. The important thing is to have these tools on hand when the power goes out because your power driven tools will run out of power quickly.

Handheld tools that you use around your house will be especially helpful after an EMP attack. A Swiss Army knife or multi-tool is portable enough to carry in your pocket or on your belt and has several useful tools in a compact design.

If you need to fix an electronic device but your soldering iron was damaged in the EMP, you can use a cordless soldering iron in its place. A butane torch comes in a plastic kit that includes a butane torch, solder dispenser, cap, clean sponge, 8mm wrench, 7mm wrench, reflector, hot blower, hot knife, chisel tip, and diagonal tip. The soldering iron will work for about an hour, and the fuel is refillable.

When stocking up your supply of tools, you want to make sure you include tools you can use to tend to your garden. For this, you will want smaller hand tools, as well as larger items such as shovels, rakes, and a wheelbarrow.

Clothing

Most people have more than enough clothing to survive any situation for a long time. If you take a close look at most closets, they are packed full.

Just remember, in a post-EMP world you will be participating in a variety of outside activities, like working in a garden, gathering water or wood, so it is important to be mindful of what you are wearing and what you will be required to do in a post-EMP world.

When it comes to preparing your clothing, it is important to remember that you will no longer have central heat or air in your home, which means it will stay hotter or cooler depending on where you live. You will need to have clothing for both extremes of temperature.

Make sure you have plenty of sleeping bags and blankets to keep warm after the sun goes down because no matter where you live, once the sun goes down things will cool off.

If you live in an area with harsh winters, having extra blankets and sleeping bags will be even more important for your survival. Make sure to have plenty of extreme cold weather clothing and dress in loose-fitting layers.

Be cognizant of children, babies, and elders as their body temperatures vary from yours. Be sure to keep the proper clothing handy to ensure they remain comfortable throughout the situation.

Bug Out Bag (Just In Case)

If your house becomes unfit for habitation, or you need to leave in a hurry, you need to have a "Bug Out Bag" ready, so you can just grab it and go.

A bug out bag is a backpack or other sturdy nylon bag that is geared with items that you will need to survive that you can quickly grab and go on your way out the door if you are forced to leave quickly.

Every member of your family needs to have their bag with their name clearly labeled on the outside of the bag. Having each family member carry their own bag is important because you can't carry everything that your family will need in the event of a severe emergency. If you have toddlers and babies, you will need to have a bag for them as well. While they can't carry the bags themselves, having all their items together in one place will make it easier for you to take care of their needs quickly.

Everyone else in the family, including children and teenagers, can carry their own backpacks. The sizes and weights of the bags will vary, and it is essential that they are all waterproof. You will want to try and find backpacks that come with pockets that they can access without taking the bag off.

Survival Food for Your Backpack

Having to leave your house quickly, doesn't mean you will be required to eat low quality, cardboard-tasting food. These days you can dine on gourmet meals in the post-EMP world. There are some companies where you can purchase gourmet food that will last for a few days, a week, or even for months at a time.

A great option for your backpack is freeze dried foods. Freeze dried foods lock in the nutrients and taste. When you're ready to eat the meals, you just have to re-hydrate them, usually by adding hot water.

The military uses MREs (Meals Ready to Eat) to feed their soldiers when they are unable to get back to the mess hall. MREs are another option of food for your bug out bag. MREs only need to be heated, making them heavier than freeze dried food. If soldiers are out on a long range foot patrol, they are given LRPs or Long Range Patrol Rations. These are cube-shaped freeze dried meals that are vacuum-packed, making them an easier option to pack in your survival bag. They only weigh on average, 5oz each before being rehydrated, and once they are rehydrated, you have a 21oz hot meal with more meat on average than the normal freeze dried meals.

What Goes In a Bug Out Bag

Before an EMP attack, you will want to take the time to decide on a bug out destination and pre-plan the route you will take to reach the destination. You will need to figure out how much food and other essentials you will need. To figure out how much food and other essentials that you will need, you will need to estimate how many miles the slowest member of your group can travel in a day. Use this number to calculate the number of days you will be on the road and pack your bags accordingly.

Adults that are in shape should carry **no more than 20 to 25 percent of their body weight**. This weight will be much less for children, the elderly, and overweight individuals. If you are traveling on foot, you will not be able to carry everything that you will need, which makes hiding provisions along your route necessary. This will help keep the weight each person has to carry to a minimum.

When planning for a quick exit, it is important to be prepared and make sure everyone is on the same page. Everyone in the group needs to have a sturdy and comfortable pack. You may be on the road for several days, so having a pack that is comfortable is necessary. It is also important that everyone in your group is wearing well, broken-in footwear. Having footwear that is broken in will help to avoid injury, chafing, or blisters. Be sure to stop if anyone in your group is getting a sore spot inside their boot. It is essential to treat blisters before they become severe.

If your route requires hiking through rough terrain or entails long downhill stretches, it is important for everyone in your group to have their toe nails trimmed. To help prevent falls and make backpacking easier, a pair of trekking poles would be a good investment. They can also double as adjustable poles when pitching your shelter.

Carrying all of the water you will need during your trip may not be practical, so you should try and plan a route that has a water source along the way. Bring along a canteen and water bladders, a water filter and water disinfection chemicals so you can collect water for the days ahead.

Did you Know?

Many canteens that you can buy nest with a cup and a stove so you can heat or boil water to make hot drinks in cold weather. The heated water can also be used to rehydrate freeze dried or dehydrated food. Some of these canteens also have small pockets on the side of their cover where you can store a lighter, fuel tablet and water disinfection tablets or packets.

Besides finding water along your route, you will also need to have a way to cook food and boil water. There are basic all- in-one cooking kits available that are perfect for cooking out in the open and lightweight pots that you can use to cook over a campfire.

When it comes to packing clothing, it's best to pack at least one or two extra sets of clothes in case your clothing gets wet. Choose clothing that will dry quickly. If you live in an area with colder temperatures, don't wear a layer of cotton next to your skin. Cotton will absorb your sweat and hold it next to your skin and can cause you to become hypothermic. The best thing to wear in cold weather is a polypropylene base layer with a wool outer layer. While high-tech synthetic fabrics are lightweight, they don't last as long. You will need to find a balance between natural fibers and synthetic materials. Along with wearing a pair of hiking boots for your journey, you should also pack a light pair of tennis shoes for times when you are walking on a relatively flat surface.

Most areas will cool off in the evenings, even in the summer. Make sure to pack long pants, long-sleeved shirts, and other clothing that will keep you warm during the chilly nights. This type of clothing is also good for keeping the sun off your skin on hot days. They will also protect you from being eaten alive by pests such as mosquitoes.

Along with an extra set of clothing, pack extra underwear and socks. If you are traveling on foot, you want to change your socks frequently to prevent blisters, trench foot, athlete's foot and other fungal infections. Changing into dry clothes will help keep you warm. A 100 percent cotton bandana is useful to have in your pack and has a variety of uses from first aid application to making char cloth.

A poncho is a great item to have in your bug out bag as it has many uses aside from keeping you protected from the rain. It can be used as a make-shift tent or overhead shelter or ground cloth or improvised bivouac sack to protect your sleeping bag or blanket from ground moisture or dew. Choosing items for your pack that have multiple uses will help cut down on the weight. Practice your survival skills before you need them by going backpacking and camping. You can work on your skills and test your equipment to make sure everything will function properly when needed.

The sun can quickly deplete your energy if you're not careful. Finding ways to protect yourself from the sun is an important measure to take when preparing your bug out bag. Before you leave the house, grab a hat to keep the sun off your head and the rain out of your face. A pair of sunglasses is also an important item to have as they will protect your eyes from being exposed to the sun for long periods of time. Having a good pair of sunglasses is especially important if you will be traveling in snow, to prevent snow blindness and on the water to protect your eyes from the reflected light.

When it comes to packing a shelter, you can pack a lightweight tent or bring along a tarp with rope. Research sleeping bags to find the lightest in weight that will still keep you warm. While the down material is much lighter, if it gets wet, it will lose a lot of its insulating properties. You also want to invest in a good sleeping pad to insulate your body from conductive heat loss from sleeping on the ground. Also, make sure you have enough emergency blankets for your entire group.

Each person needs to have their individual personal hygiene items and medications they need, and a first aid kit is an essential part of a bug out bag. You will also need to have waterproof matches as well as an accelerant so you can build a fire at night to cook your food and help your group keep warm. Each person should have basic survival gear in their pockets, so they never become separated from them. Make sure you have a flashlight or headlamp, rechargeable batteries, and a portable solar battery charger.

If your route takes you along a stream or river, a small fishing kit will allow you to catch fish for lunches or dinners. The Swiss Army knife or multi-tool knife mentioned earlier will allow you to clean and gut the fish before cooking.

A way to stay informed during your trek is by bringing a small, battery-powered, emergency radio. These don't take up much room and are a great way to keep up-to-date on the latest information about the post-EMP world. If you have them, you should also carry two-way radios so your group can stay in contact with each other if you should find it necessary to split up.

Your route may contain some foliage that you may need to clear away. Pack sturdy gloves and a machete, small ax, hatchet or tomahawk for this type of situation. It will make clearing out foliage and debris easier. You will also want to pack a small folding shovel, entrenching tool, or trowel and some toilet paper to dig a hole for waste disposal.

Finally, pack your important papers and data and make sure to bring a weapon with you to protect you and your family. Consider bringing a firearm along with extra ammo, your identification, and your concealed carry weapon permit if you have one. Bring pepper spray as well for situations that don't require the use of deadly force. Pepper spray can also be handy if you encounter any unfriendly dogs or other animals along your route.

These documents will be important if you find yourself in a situation where you can't return to your home. If your neighborhood has been declared a disaster area, you may not be able to get back into your neighborhood without the proper identification. During an emergency, people become afraid of looters or outsiders that may potentially be carrying a disease. If you can prove you belong there, you will have an easier time getting back to your home.

Fire

Knowing how to start a fire is essential during the time of a disaster. Your supply of matches will eventually run out leaving you helpless if you don't have the knowledge of how to start a fire. Starting a fire without the use of matches isn't as easy as it looks, and everybody in your group needs to know the "primitive" fire starting methods.

The preparation is the key to building a fire. The first thing you need to do is gather plenty of wood. Before you begin, you want to clear the area of all flammable materials to avoid starting any unwanted fires. Have a bucket of water, or pile of dirt, nearby in case you need to put the fire out in a hurry.

The first thing you need to do is start with a "bird's nest" of tinder, and then add enough kindling to fill both your hands when they are placed together in a circle. Finally, add three big bundles of firewood. If you want your fire to last all night, your fire circle should be the size of a circle you can make with your arms if you were to hug a tree.

When you leave the area, it is important to make sure the fire is completely out and cool to the touch. If there are any embers left smoldering they can easily be coaxed back to life by the wind, potentially igniting a wildfire.

During your preparation, familiarize yourself with the most common types of fire pits and lays. There are fires that can keep you warm all night, ones that are more effective producers of light, and ones that are better at reflecting the warmth and ones that are better for cooking. A Dakota Fire Pit is effective for both cooking and keeping you warm. The fire it produces is also harder to see and produces very little smoke.

A great resource for starting fires in less than ideal situations is a cotton ball coated with petroleum jelly. The cotton ball burns for several minutes giving your tinder and kindling time to catch fire. You can also pre-soak twigs in lighter fluid and store them away from the heat for use at a later date.

For a waterproof option, you can purchase chemical tinder tablets of gel fuels. These are small, lightweight alternatives and will burn even if they get wet. Trioxane, Hexamine, Esbit Tablets, Tinder Tablets, and Wet Fire Tables are some of the most popular kinds.

For an even sturdier alternative to matches, you can purchase a metal match or ferrocerium rod. These are made out of metals and rare earth minerals and will survive everything from damp air to a dunk in the creek. You can also use Ferro rods and magnesium blocks to shave into small piles of tinder. These types of fire starting products won't ever go bad, but there is the potential that you will wear them out. When you strike the Ferro rods with a carbide striker or high carbon steel, they are the most effective. Avoid using a low carbon stainless steel striker as it doesn't throw enough of a spark to start a fire. If you decide that this is the way you want to go, be sure to purchase several of these because you don't ever want to run into a situation where you aren't able to start a fire.

ALTERNATIVES FOR POWER, COMMUNICATION AND TRANSPORT

Power

After an EMP event, there will be no way to restore the electrical grid. Thus the only remaining options are alternative types of energy. This is when solar energy and wind energy comes in useful. Using these two resources will help you make use of your electronics. You can do this by recharging deep cycle batteries that can last for up to seven days.

Solar power is a very good alternative to gasoline. With no electricity, the tankers that are fueled with gasoline won't work because they need pumps controlling the pipelines that work only with the help of an electrical infrastructure.

Solar panel electricity systems capture the sun's energy. Basically, it converts the sunlight into electricity, which can be used to run an entire household. These solar panels don't need direct sunlight to work as they can still generate some electricity on a cloudy day. The solar power is accumulated into a deep cycle battery that recharges batteries, lights and other useful appliances.

Solar panels are good and money saving investments; you can buy for less than $500, alongside with battery charges. For charging basic electronics such as: communication equipment, LED lights and recharging batteries. It is recommended to use 12 volt solar panels. Ventilation is required for full efficiency, specifically during summertime.

Wind power means simply converting wind into electrical power. Wind has become a noticeable contributor to our energy mix. It has become a major source of electricity around the world. Wind energy requires turbines, or windmills. However, wind is not as accessible of a resource as the sun is. For example, during the summer turbines can produce less power than during the winter (when there are stronger winds). Thus, windmills become fully efficient when wind speed is over 6.5m/s.

Despite all, wind turbines are a little more expensive to manage and repair, than solar panels. Wind turbines have electronic components, which mean that these wind generator systems have higher chances to be affected by an EMP. This is why, when preparing, you should stockpile electronic spare parts for your wind generators.

To be fully covered, many experts suggest that the solar and wind systems can be used simultaneous in order to produce energy in any type of weather.

Human powered electricity is another innovative way to produce energy by using basic electronic equipment. Pedaling a stationary bicycle powered generator to produce energy is a great work-out. In order to receive the right amount of electricity you will need to pedal at least two hours every day. The cost for a bicycle powered generator can be up to $500.

A less expensive option is a hand generator, costing between $50 and $200. The option doubles the amount of time invested in creating energy.

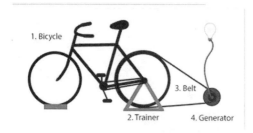 

Communication

When preparing for an EMP event, it is important to consider how you will communicate and get in touch with your family and loved ones.

This is why it is important to make sure that you develop a well-established correspondence system.

It is important to include your family or group in the preparing arrangements by discussing with them about the importance of establishing a gathering place and time schedule; make sure that in the event of an EMP or other disaster you and your family have a spot set where everybody can meet.

A Personal Beacon Locator (PBL) will help you locate your family and keep in touch with them.

These locators send out predefined messages to the person of interest.

Remember to make a stockpile of Personal Beacon Locators and keep them safe from an EMP, in a Faraday container (immediately after the electromagnetic pulse) and in another sealed galvanized containers.

Considering that these locators work solely on batteries, it is important to remove the batteries before storing them in order to prevent the damage of the devices.

Radio transceivers are also very useful in the aftermath of an EMP event. It will help you keep in touch with friends and other members of the family or group.

In a radio transceiver, the receiver is silenced while transmitting. An electronic switch allows the transmitter and receiver to be connected to the same antenna.

In order to prevent them from being

damaged, do not forget to remove the antenna and batteries and store them inside a secure container. Moreover, store extra rechargeable batteries and make sure you have an alternative power supply, such as solar panels.

Following an EMP, telephones, cell phones and internet will no longer work. Two way radios will become a valuable tool for individuals. This is why it is important to prepare with communication equipment and protect them from the effect of an EMP.

Transport

After a EMP attack, lifestyle of modern society will change drastically. It will begin to collapse; infrastructures and law enforcements will be less available to help you in emergency situations.

One strategy in the event of an electromagnetic pulse is evacuation. This could be to a secure location that you previously prepared.

Getting to a location or a less populated area can be a difficult mission. All modern cars have electronic components to operate, thus they will be completely useless after the EMP.

Bug out Vehicle

If you have a vehicle that will still run, this is the option you want to choose. Walking to a bug-out location should be a last resort. If you want to be able to use a vehicle, you need to leave soon enough to avoid the massive levels of road congestion that will occur when people realize the gravity of the situation. With a vehicle, you may be able to use back roads or 4x4 trails that are free of accidents and vehicles that are disabled or have run out of fuel. Having a bug-out vehicle will allow you to travel distances that would take you weeks on foot in a matter of hours.

When choosing your bug-out vehicle(s), you want to be sure they are large enough to carry everyone in your group, their bags, and plenty of supplies to get you to your destination.

Having a drivable vehicle after an EMP attack and making sure you have enough fuel to make the trip to your bug-out destination are **primary concerns.**

A vehicle with a high-capacity fuel tank or extra tanks will increase the area you can cover and eliminate your need to carry large amounts of fuel in gas cans. You may want to carry Jerry Cans or fuel dollies in a hitch mounted cargo carrier to keep your passengers safe from dangerous and smelly fuel.

Your primary concern after an EMP attack is having a reliable bug-out vehicle that is well-maintained. Older vehicles have a better chance of working after the EMP attack. Depending on the year of the car, the vehicle may have a key system that could be damaged by an EMP. It is important for you to identify these systems early and learn how to replace them. You also want to purchase replacement parts and keep them stored in a Faraday cage.

There have been very few unclassified EMP tests performed on automobiles. The testing assumed a maximum field strength of 50 kV/m. They were stopped at a much lower field strength when vehicles began manifesting problems. Classified super-EMP weapons have the potential to yield field strengths in excess of 50 kV/m. **Note: the newest model vehicle tested with the unclassified EMP were in 2003. Newer vehicles will have more problems due to their heavier reliance on microelectronics. There have also been no unclassified EMP automobile tests done to date with an actual nuclear weapons detonated at high a altitude.** There is no way to know how much damaged today's vehicles will take, especially at higher field strengths.

There are also other factors that figure into the equation, like whether or not your vehicle is running at the time, what materials were used in the construction of your garage, how much of the car's body is conductive, and the orientation of your vehicle relative to where the EMP is detonated. While your vehicle may survive an EMP attack and work just fine, it is better to be prepared and do everything you can to turn the odds in your favor.

Systems of a car the may be damaged by an EMP:

- Electronic fuel injection
- Anti-lock braking system

- Electronic ignition
- Starting motor
- Ignition coil
- Mechanical distributor (can be replaced with points)
- Alternator or Generator
- All computers needed to make the vehicle run (in newer vehicles)

To be safe, if your vehicle has any of these components, you should store shielded extras. If you have the means, you should consider the requirements needed for a bug-out vehicle and purchase a vehicle that you can fix up the way you want.

If you want to be able to carry more supplies to your bug-out location, you may want to consider purchasing a trailer. The only consideration you need to take is whether the vehicle/trailer combination can safely travel the route you've planned to your bug-out location.

Here is a list of attributes that would make for a good bug-out vehicle:

- Older model year (roughly 1986 or older) with as few EMP- sensitive parts as possible and that are more easily repaired.
- Long-range fuel tanks, extra fuel tanks
- High clearance 4x4
- Tow package and trailer or hitch-mounted cargo carrier
- Bull bar type bumper
- Off road lighting
- Plenty of cargo space
- Communications gear
- Full-size spare tire
- Off road or all-terrain tires (with run-flat donuts installed in them if you can afford them)
- Winch/air compressor combo with QD air hose and

adapters
- Second battery
- Extrication gear/tow straps/chains/shovel/ax/saw
- Non-electric fuel pump and hoses to pump gas (B&D Jack Rabbit of similar)
- Rooftop cargo rack, tie-down straps, cargo pod, mounting brackets for tools and steps, grab handles or ladders to reach it
- Rear bumper with swing out for Jerry cans, water cans, spare tire, hi-lift jack
- Repair kit: tools, spare parts, tire patch kit, jumper cables, fluids, belts, etc.

Horse

In a post-EMP world, horses have numerous uses. Without electricity or gasoline, a horse can be a versatile mode of transportation and a substitute for various tools.

Traveling by horse is much faster than walking. You can also travel off the road where vehicles aren't able to go. With the addition of wagons or buggies, using a horse to transport you and your family to your bug-out location can be extremely useful.

Using horses to lead a train of packhorses, mules, and donkeys is a great idea. They can transport quite a bit of gear to inaccessible locations, and they can survive largely on forage and water.

Bicycle

If you don't already know how to ride a bike, it's time to learn. The means of transportation will be a major concern after an EMP, and being able to get around on a bike will be a lot more appealing than walking on foot. Vehicles and trailers can also carry bicycles, or you can purchase a folding bicycle and place it on a rack. Having a bicycle prevents you from becoming stranded and being forced to walk on foot. When you purchase a bike, be sure to purchase spare parts, tubes, patch kits and tires to keep your bicycle in working order. If you are planning on using your bicycle as your backup mode of transportation, you may want to consider building or buying a trailer for your bicycle. This way, you can carry a greater load without throwing your bicycle off balance.

Another way of moving from one place to another, which can be very useful in case on an EMP event, is building simple means of transportation on water such as rafts, barges and kayaks. You can make them on your own using wood and basic construction supplies. These means of transport can prove very useful, if you are living near water such as rivers and lakes.

How to build a simple raft

The best part is that rafts can be built from just about everything; what a raft is built from depends on the materials that you have available.Materials that can be used for rafts include: logs, gallon drums or containers, inner tubes, sealed boxes, used bottles or cans and just about anything that floats.

The structure that creates the platform and holds the floatation together for most rafts, is generally made from wood, but you can also use metal or even plastic. However, the most popular choice for a raft frame is lumber, plywood and even pallet wood.

1.   The first thing you have to do is collect logs. The number of the logs used, depends on how big you want your raft to be. Be careful to choose equal size logs so that they can fit together better.

2.   Collect other wood poles that are longer than the logs. Put a pole at top end of the bunched up logs. Use two poles crisscrossed under the logs, and a final log along the bottom edge. Repeat the process with the remaining poles. Verify that there are no big gaps between the logs, otherwise they will take in water.

3.   Tie very tightly the ends of the poles at each end to clamp the logs. You can use strong vines and rope or plants which may provide you with strong fastening.

4.   Use planks, driftwood or tree bark to lay them on the top sides of the poles in order to make an even platform.

WHAT YOU NEED TO REMEMBER

Although it cannot harm the human body, an EMP event can have devastating effects upon our modern society; the electromagnetic pulses will cause the circuits to overburden, melting away any conductors and disabling any electrical systems and devices.

In aftermath of an EMP the world around you can easily be characterized by attacks, robberies, car crashes and other unpleasant incidents. The first thing that would go down is the power grid. This can lead to a total blackout, as the street lights will no longer be sustained by electricity. As we might imagine, this will intensify human attacks.

It is very important to consider our safety when it comes to a survival situation of this kind. With no street lights and no traffic light systems, car crashes will intensify and people will be begin to panic trying to make sure their loved ones are safe. For this reason, in the event of an EMP, you should pay very close attention to road traffic.

Stepping outside of your safety area can be dangerous. This is why it is very important to include your entire family or group in the prepping arrangements, especially when it comes to personal safety. For example, teach your children self-defense techniques in case they fall victims to attacks or how to read a compass and find their way wherever they are.

Another thing that you should always remember is that, with chaos all around and limited resources, you need to be very careful. Be sure to explain to your family or group the consequences of traveling alone, especially at nightfall. You need to avoid becoming easy targets for the possible attackers.

Crowded urban areas are a bad place to be in, when an EMP strikes. If you find yourself in a place like this, then you and your family members should evacuate and pack essential supplies, like water, food, blankets, candles, compass, maps, whistle, first aid kit, metal cups, clothes and matches.

Don't forget about the flashlights, as they are very useful in survival situations; you can send SOS messages in Morse code: first make three short flashes (S). Then, make three longer ones (O). Finally, flash the light again in three brief movements (S).

Another thing you need to remember is that, along with hospitals, police stations, and other infrastructures, the banking systems will also be heavily affected by an EMP blast. Bank robberies will increase as thieves can no longer be stopped by law enforcements and security systems.

ATMs and computers will no longer functions, so withdrawing money from the bank or making online payments are not an option. As a result, the whole economy will be affected and this can lead to a complete financial collapse.

Chaos and panic will be the dominant atmosphere among our society. Crime rates will increase, as the telephones and radio lines will no longer work. Because of this, emergency services such as ambulance, firefighters or law enforcements cannot respond in time for an emergency. Therefore, the electrical disturbance made by and electromagnetic pulse will threaten everyone, from government officials to civilian groups.

In the event of an EMP, our modern civilization and life is at great risk. There will be little help from authorities. This is why it is important to start preparing on your own, so that you and your family will be safe and ready for life in the post EMP world.

SECRETS TO KEEPING CLEAN AND SANITARY AFTER THE FALL

What is sanitary really? Is it keeping a clean house or is it washing your hands before you eat? The CDC (Centers for Disease Control) has come up with their definition of sanitation and how you should think of it when you think of your home or environment.

Basic sanitation is described as having access to facilities for the safe disposal of human waste (feces and urine), as well as having the ability to maintain hygienic conditions, through services such as garbage collection, industrial/hazardous waste management, and waste water treatment and disposal.

In today's world, we don't think too much about personal hygiene or sanitation. When the dishes are dirty, we wash them. When we need to use the bathroom, we do so and then flush it away. When we are dirty, we shower. When you are thirsty, you turn on the tap and get a nice, cold drink of water. Some even put filters on their already clean tap water to make it taste a little better.

All of these are luxuries we take for granted. After a major collapse, basic sanitation and hygiene will become a serious issue. Nearly any disaster scenario ends up interrupting the water supply.

Without power to run pumps and sanitation systems, water will be non-existent or unclean and not safe to drink or use. Even the most basic things like flushing the toilet will vanish when the water supply is cut off.

Preppers often get caught up in the storing of food and water and don't think about the consequences of a true disaster.

We have to practice good sanitation and hygiene in order to remain healthy. Think about some of the third world countries that battle illnesses that can be blamed on poor sanitation.

It is crucial a prepper sits down and comes up with a plan for sanitation after SHTF. Knowing what to do to keep your family clean and living in sanitary conditions could very well mean the difference between life and death.

Once you have read through all the different aspects of sanitation, you can start prepping items that will make sure your living space is sanitary and relatively free of diseases.

Clean Water

Most preppers are aware of the fact that water is essential to life. You cannot go more than a couple of days without clean drinking water. This is why preppers store water. Clean, potable water is also necessary for basic hygiene and cleaning purposes. You don't want to use "dirty" water to wash dishes or your body. Dirty water doesn't always look dirty. In fact, it can be crystal clear and still be filled with harmful disease, bacteria and chemicals.

You will need hundreds of gallons of water to carry you through a month or two. If you have the space to do this, go for it! It will certainly increase your odds of survival. If you want to bottle your own water to save money, that is an option. However, avoid flimsy milk jugs. The plastic is thin and will break down in a matter of months leaving you with a mess and no water. Use old juice bottles and water bottles instead. They will hold up much longer.

Another option you should invest in is something called a water bob. They are fairly inexpensive and can be found on the internet. The device is a large bladder that fits into the bathtub. At the first sign of trouble, you fill the bob up and let it rest in the tub. It keeps the water clean and free of debris that could fall into the tub. Building swimming pools or backyard ponds is another trick many preppers have employed.

While storing water is a great idea, it isn't really a long-term solution. If a disaster was big enough, it could have you living without running water for months or even years. You need a renewable source of water that you can clean and make safe to use for sanitation and drinking. If you have your own property, having your own well is your best option.

This is a large expense up front and you will need to be in an area that has good ground water, but it is worth it. In most disaster scenarios, the well water would remain clean, unless you were dealing with an earthquake situation. This could cause the well to be contaminated with debris.

Rain barrels and cisterns designed to catch rainwater are another favorite among preppers. There are plenty of ways you can make your own rain catchment system at your house. It is very inexpensive and easily set up.

The local lake, river or stream may work for a bit, but it will quickly become a hot spot for other survivors, which can get dicey. These sources of water are also not safe to use without being treated first.

The idea is to have several options. The prepper mindset is to have a backup for your backup and maybe even another backup, just in case.

Filtering Water

A rule of thumb that every prepper and survivor should follow is this;

All water is dirty until purified.

There are several means of purifying water, but filtering is typically the first step. If you are using water that isn't clear, you will want to remove as much of the sediment as possible. This is a fairly simple process.

Filtering Water

A rule of thumb that every prepper and survivor should follow is this;

All water is dirty until purified.

There are several means of purifying water, but filtering is typically the first step. If you are using water that isn't clear, you will want to remove as much of the sediment as possible. This is a fairly simple process.

1.   Pour the water into a container and allow it to sit for until all the sediment sinks to the bottom.

2.   Skim off all the material that is floating off the top.

3.   Carefully pour the water into another container, being careful not to stir up the sediment on the bottom.

4.   Pour the water into your filtering system and then purify.

You can of course pour the water filled with sediment directly into your filtering system, but it will break down your filter faster.

Another option is to pour the water through several layers of cloth. A bandana or old t-shirt works great.

If you suspect that are chemical contaminants in the water, add a piece of charcoal to the water to absorb the chemicals. Boiling the water will kill bacteria and parasites, but it will not remove chemicals.

You can find a number of different water filters on the market. Do your best to find one with the greatest filtration. Some protozoa and bacteria are super tiny. The smaller the micron filtration, the better the filter.

Solar Disinfection

Solar disinfection, often referred to as SODIS, is another option. The sun can be used to treat your water and reduce or eliminate the dangers of protozoa, bacteria and viruses that may be in the water.

You will need to use plastics that are BPA free.

Shake the water to oxygenate it and put it on the roof or another area that gets full sun.

Allow the sun to heat the water for at least six hours. If it is cloudy, the water should be left in the sun for 2 days.

Chemical Disinfection

There are numerous chemical disinfectants you can use. Iodine, chlorine bleach and hydrogen peroxide are the most popular. An old fashioned way is to mix water with wine to make it safe to drink. The alcohol is supposed to kill the harmful contaminants. Always have several options available to you so you always have clean drinking water on hand.

Personal Hygiene

You may assume that because the world has gone sideways, your personal hygiene isn't important. It is. In fact, you need to pay more attention to your own personal hygiene and the sanitation of your living conditions. Germs and bacteria can wreak havoc in a survival situation.

You cannot afford to become ill or pick up a nasty bug because sanitation is lacking.

Getting sick with a stomach bug in a survival situation is much different than it is today. You will battle dehydration and be unable to keep up with the physical duties needed to stay alive. Your best medicine for illness is prevention. Make hygiene a top concern and do your best to avoid getting sick.

Staying Clean

Our mothers have drilled it into our heads since the time we could walk. Wash your hands before you eat! Now, we know we should wash our hands throughout the day and most especially before we touch our face, eat, after using the restroom or handling anything that is likely carrying germs. Germs are everywhere! Door handles, keyboards, faucets and so on. You have to make a real effort to keep your hands clean. If you forget or just don't wash your hands after any activity, you are dramatically increasing your risk of becoming extremely ill.

The following are some of the methods you can use to clean your hands. Your hands are on the front lines so to speak and are like magnets for germs. Keep them clean!

Soap and Water

Soap and water is still the go-to source for cleaning your hands. You don't have to get a fancy, anti-bacterial soap to be effective. Especially avoid soap that has triclosan in it. This harsh cleanser can actually weaken your skin, which leave you more susceptible to infections.

Stock up on cheap soap and paper towels if you can swing it. Paper towels are more effective at keeping your hands free of germs. Towels will work, but they harbor bacteria. You could end up drying your clean hands with a germ-infested towel. Yes paper towels may seem wasteful, if you are dealing with an outbreak of some virus or illness, take the plunge and use paper towels to dry your hands after washing.

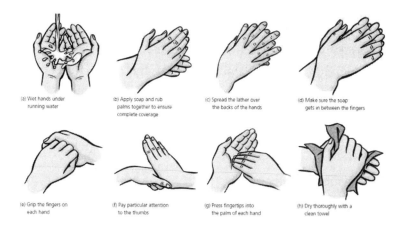

(a) Wet hands under running water

(b) Apply soap and rub palms together to ensure complete coverage

(c) Spread the lather over the backs of the hands

(d) Make sure the soap gets in between the fingers

(e) Grip the fingers on each hand

(f) Pay particular attention to the thumbs

(g) Press fingertips into the palm of each hand

(h) Dry thoroughly with a clean towel

Hot Water

If you don't have soap, scrubbing your hands under hot water will do. Get the water as hot as you can stand it and rub between the fingers and the backs of your hands.

It may not seem effective, but the hot water will kill some germs and remove quite a bit of the rest.

Hand Sanitizer

Hand sanitizer should not be substituted for soap and water if it is available. However, if water is scarce a drop or two of hand sanitizer will go a long way to cleaning your hands. Typically, you would apply hand sanitizer as another measure of protection after you have washed your hands with soap and water, but you can use it alone if it is all that is available.

Hand sanitizer is not magical and will not destroy every little germ or virus that your hands come into contact with. It is typically 99.99% effective. It cannot kill things like e. coli, MRSA (staph) or the flu virus.

Just because you use sanitizer after coming into contact with one of these contagions, it doesn't mean you are protected.

Hand sanitizer is largely made up of alcohol, which can dry your hands out with regular usage. Dry hands lead to cracked hands which increase your risk of contracting an illness. If you are using sanitizer often throughout the **day, use one that has very little alcohol content. For sporadic use, the high alcohol content will be okay.**

Baby Wipes/Wet Wipes

If you have sticky hands or a little dirt, wet wipes are a great option. Wet wipes tend to have alcohol in them, which will help eliminate germs. As mentioned above, alcohol can be rough on your skin if used a lot. Baby wipes are another option and many brands do not have alcohol. This is an excellent option if you just need to wipe your hands off.

 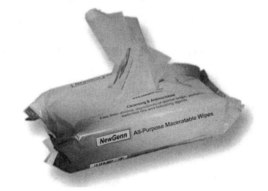

Clean Nails

Do what you can to keep your nails clean. Packing a manicure set in your emergency preps isn't about vanity, it is about sanitation. Under the nails is a prime place for germs to hang out. When washing your hands, make sure you scrub under the nails. Keep your nails trip and in good shape so they are easier to clean and work with.

Gloves

Do yourself a favor and wear gloves anytime you are caring for anybody that is sick.

This will help cut down on the transmission of germs and viruses.

This will cut down on how frequently you have to wash your hands as well, although, you should still wash them before and after putting on gloves, you don't need to be quite as vigorous. Wearing gloves to take care of certain cleaning activities can also add a layer of protection, just in case soap and water doesn't do the trick.

Human Excrement

Human waste and excrement is a fact of life. It is not one of those things anybody really like to think about or talk about, but it is a serious issue that must be addressed. Excrement, i.e. vomit, snot and sputum and of course feces, all needs to be properly disposed of to ensure nobody is sickened by the bacteria that lurks in these things.

Clean hands is your best method of prevention. If you touch any human waste or excrement, a thorough hand washing is in order. In ancient cultures, people would use one hand for eating and the other to take care of business below in order to avoid any cross contamination.

What You Shouldn't Do

Don't let it pile up and absolutely do not leave it exposed. Flies will dine on the waste, which will likely contain things like the very nasty and potentially fatal e. coli. Flies and mosquitoes will transmit the disease.

Cholera is a common problem with these exposed excrement piles. It can quickly wipe out an entire community. Always cover the waste.

Uncovered holes or cesspools are never a good idea.

Back in the 60s, a group of people decided to get back to nature and lived together in a commune. It wasn't long before dysentery swept through the small community. The outbreak was blamed on an open latrine.

In a later section, we will go into the various ways you can take care of business without making anybody sick.

Women's Hygiene

Women will have to deal with personal hygiene issues that involve their menstruation cycle. Without drug stores to run to, all women should have a healthy supply of feminine products on hand. These will actually be in high demand after the fall and will be a valuable bartering item. Proper hygiene is essential.

Ideally, reusable items like the Diva Cup or cloths that can be washed and reused are best. These silicone cups are reusable for up to ten years. Of course, it is absolutely crucial the cups are washed thoroughly in between uses. You will have a hard time finding these after disaster strikes, so it is best to pick up a few today. They will also be in high demand and will be valuable in the bartering world. Disposable items are convenient, but they will run out eventually.

Baby Care

Taking care of the youngest survivors means you will need to think about their hygiene. Diapers will be a major concern. Even if a toddler has been potty trained, the stress of a situation could result in soiled underwear.

Storing disposable diapers is an excellent idea. It doesn't have to be the premium diapers.

The cheap ones will be better than nothing at all. Diapers will be another premium item in the bartering world.

Because disposable diapers will mean more trash and because they will run out, it is also a good idea to store cloth diapers.

Cloth diapers are versatile and can be used for more than just diapering. Flat fold cloth diapers are your best option. They are easily washed and will grow with the child. They also dry much quicker.

Another throwback to the old days that was used when children were around was to section off a space for kids.

The kids would be allowed to run diaper free. Kids of similar ages would be sectioned off together.

This idea has merit, but you must consider little ones who like to put their hands in their mouths. This could end in illness if mobile kids were put in the same area with infants.

Dental Care

Getting a major toothache or something as serious as an abcessed tooth in a survival situation is a big deal. You can prevent a lot of dental issues by practicing good dental hygiene. Add toothpaste and toothbrushes to your emergency supplies. They are very inexpensive and take up very little space, but are so valuable!

If you don't have toothpaste or a brush, you can use an old-fashioned trick known as twig chewing. This involves chewing on a branch from an aromatic tree until it becomes stringy. Use the frayed twig to brush your teeth. It will leave you with a fresh feeling.

Hair Care

Your hair needs to be kept clean. It isn't about vanity, it is about being sanitary. Unkempt hair can lead to lice or fleas. This is an itchy, uncomfortable situation that can result in excessive itching that leads to sores, which leads to infection. If you cannot keep up with washing your hair on a regular basis, cut it off.

If you don't have soap and water, a mud treatment will do. Cake mud on your scalp and hair. Allow it to dry and then brush it out or remove it with your hands.

Body Care

If the weather is mild and not too cold, bathe daily if you can. Think of your body like your hands. You want it to be as clean and germ-free as possible. If you have the water to spare, bathe frequently. If the temperatures are chilly or water is scarce, take sponge baths.

This gives you a chance to look for ticks and other parasites. You can't afford to be sickened. Personal hygiene is the best defense against infection and germs. Being clean will go a long way to making you feel better and keeping you healthy.

Toilets

You need to be able to dispose of your human waste effectively without leaving it exposed to critters and pests that will end up using it to spread disease. The following are some of the toilet options you may have or can construct. Each has its own pros and cons.

Camper Toilets

Camper toilets are great and so much like the real thing. You do your business and then flush. However, these are not long term solutions. They will only work for a few days or weeks, depending on your holding tank.

Bucket Toilets

The bucket toilet is a favorite among preppers. It is a 5-gallon bucket lined with a heavy-duty garbage bag (don't use the cheap bags!).

Add a bit of water or cat litter to the bottom of the bag to help cut down on odor.

Adding a handful of sawdust or litter once somebody uses the bucket will help keep it a little cleaner as well.

When the bag is about half-full or to the capacity of the bag strength, remove the bag. Bury the full trash bags to keep them from being torn open by animals. It is a good idea to have two buckets. One for urine and another for feces.

Composting Toilets

You can make your own compost toilet or buy one already made. It is essentially the same concept at the bucket toilet. A little sawdust and time and the waste is transformed into compost. These are ideal because you need very little, if any, water to keep them operable and the odor controlled.

Outhouse/Latrine

An outhouse is an option if you are handy with a hammer and nails and a shovel. However, you need to have sawdust, dirt or lime on hand. Every time somebody uses the toilet, sprinkle a bit over the top to keep those flies at bay.

Toilet Paper

You don't realize how precious toilet paper is until you don't have it. Stock up on the good stuff today so you never have to find out what it is like to use the bathroom without toilet paper.

If you didn't stock up on enough or it was destroyed, you do have some options. They won't be quite as pillowy soft, but they will work.

- Paper of any kind
- Leaves—make sure they are not poisonous
- Grass
- Sawdust
- Corn cobs
- Snow

If you absolutely have to, use your hand and then make sure to wash it thoroughly afterwards.

Garbage Detail

Garbage needs to be controlled. Leaving trash lying around your house or living space will attract vermin and ultimately disease. The majority of your trash can be used for compost. Compost is excellent for the garden. The trash you cannot put into the compost heap needs to sealed in strong trash bags and then buried. You don't want animals getting into it and spreading it all about. Some garbage like cardboard and paper can be burned for heat or cooking.

Pest Control

Clearing out hiding places like piles of wood and debris from around your living quarters will help reduce the population.

It is important you keep pest and vermin from invading your sleeping quarters and food supply in order to reduce disease. Think back to the Plague, which was spread by rats.

- You have a few options when it comes to pest control.
- Poison if you don't have little kids or pets that can get into it.
- Traps are another option, but you will have to get more hands on then many people would like.
- Shooting the animals one by one is an option, but it will require you to sit around for hours and use ammunition. Only use this option if it safe.

If times are desperate, the animals can be eaten. Food is food.

Setting Up a Clean Zone

Once you have taken care of all that needs to be done to make your shelter or home as contaminant free as possible, you need to keep it that way. That means you need to restrict access and continue to keep out contaminants. It may be your home, your neighborhood or an apartment building. No matter what area you are holed up in, you need to secure it.

Back in 1918, the Spanish flu was spreading like wildfire. A county in Colorado managed to prevent it from coming in by sequestration.

They barricaded the county and banned citizens from letting anybody in without following a 2-day quarantine period.

Two people died in the county. They were sisters. One of the sisters came to visit her sister who lived on an isolated ranch. She was ill and infected her sister. The county managed to successfully protect their citizens.

Unfortunately, the ban was lifted, but the flu was not eradicated.

Five months after the ban, the flu came through and claimed the lives of five young people.

You can reduce the risk of your community being infected by instituting a clean zone. Don't get carried away and try to protect an entire town or city. Keep it small and you will have a better chance of real sequestration.

You cannot possibly control what your neighbors do with their trash, but you can control how it effects your home. Do your best to eliminate any contaminants and do what you have to to sequester your home and family members.

Quarantine Zone

If you are sheltering in place or have sequestered your home or community from the rest of the world, you need to set up a quarantine zone.

This is where newcomers or those that show signs of illness or who have been exposed need to be placed. The newcomer needs to be in the quarantine zone for 48 hours or however long is necessary for symptoms to appear.

It is a good idea to set up a decontamination area for those who are coming in from the outside. They should shower thoroughly and be given new clothes and shoes to wear in the clean zone.

If you are dealing with a virus or some other illness, the clean person would go into quarantine. If you are simply just doing what you can to keep your area clean, they should be allowed to enter once you are convinced they are free of contaminants.

Sheltering In Place

Sequestration can be achieved in your house by instituting a sheltering-in-place method. This can be done by taping windows, doors and vents are sealed with plastic. Use duct tape or nails to secure the plastic over the area. This will only work if you limit the amount of times you leave and other people come in.

Supplies to Stock Today for Proper Sanitation

In order to help you with your sanitation needs, you will need some supplies. Many of these are relatively inexpensive and can be purchased in bulk.

- Hydrogen peroxide
- Disinfectant cleaners
- Rubbing alcohol
- Soap
- Iodine
- Hand sanitizer
- Bleach
- Wet wipes
- Baby wipes
- Pharmaceutical drugs
- Natural/herbal remedies
- Pet medications
- Sunscreen
- Toilet paper
- Paper towels
- Garbage bags
- Disposable gloves
- Face masks—N95
- Plastic cutlery
- Paper plates
- Diapers
- Feminine hygiene products
- Bug poison
- Plastic sheeting
- Duct tape
- Body powder/talc
- Diatomaceous earth for controlling bugs (ants, fleas, bed bugs)

Conclusion

Keeping clean may not seem important when you are dealing with a survival situation, but it truly is.

Cleanliness is extremely important to remaining healthy. You need to take more precautions in a survival situation than you would in today's world.

You won't have the luxury of doctors and hospitals. You won't be able to get a prescription for antibiotics if you contract an infection. Do what you can to protect yourself and your family and stay healthy!

WHY YOU NEED TO PREPARE FOR AN EMERGENCY

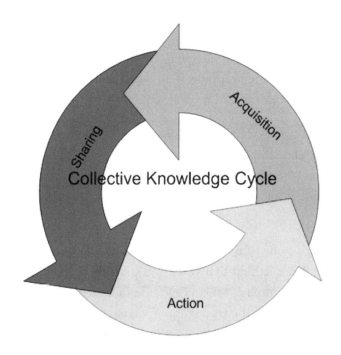

An emergency can strike at any time and leave you struggling to put food on the table, pay the bills or even be happy. Emergencies do not always come in the form of terrorist attacks or natural disasters.

The goal is to be prepared in ANY emergency—big or small. Your emergency may be the result of losing a job, a family member becoming extremely ill, a natural disaster, military conflict or the economy crashing.

You never know what is around the corner, which is why you have to be prepared for anything.

You may be on the road traveling to grandma's house, headed out on a business trip or sitting at home when disaster strikes. You won't have much time in the moment, which is why preparing now is crucial.

This world offers no guarantees. There is always something happening and it is never pretty. You don't want to be one of the people thinking, "If only I had prepared for something like this."

You will be amazed by the feeling of calm that comes over you once you have done some prepping. You won't feel as anxious about what this violent world will throw at you, because you are ready and prepared.

Disaster preparedness is a hot topic after the last few years. People are learning the hard way there are no guarantees and help is NOT always right around the corner. You may be on your own for days or weeks.

Prepping isn't one of those things you do one day and leave until you need it. It is something that you are constantly doing. Your prepping will evolve over time as you get more familiar with the idea and begin to really understand the true scope of disaster preparedness.

This book is meant to help you get all the dirty details of an emergency and how it will have a ripple effect in your life. This is key. Disaster preparedness is like pulling a string and watching what happens. You need to know what to expect so you can prepare for any eventuality.

Surviving a disaster isn't always all about the physical aspect. It is a HUGE psychological game as well. Being psychologically prepared will help you make better decisions in the moment. THIS COULD SAVE YOUR LIFE! Panic is one of leading causes of death in an emergency. Panic clouds your judgment and prevents you from making good, sound decisions.

A single thought can trigger a chain reaction. You panic and make a rash decision, which has undesirable consequences, which leads to more panic and more rash decisions. All of these quick decisions that are not thought out can lead to your demise or serious injury or heartache.

The key is to prepare NOW. Thinking about what you need, what you would do and having the supplies to follow through can truly mean the difference between life and death. This book isn't going to go into all the supplies you need to have on hand to survive. This book is going to cover the psychological preparedness aspect.

You will learn how to better manage one's thoughts, which will ultimately control your decisions as well as your overall feelings.

Understanding that some responses, emotions and feelings are normal will help you make calculated decisions on how to handle them without making your situation worse.

You will feel more confident and have more control over your situation. Knowledge is power and understanding the psychological responses that come with an emergency will give you what you need to persevere.

Survival Strategy

Your survival strategy will center on three crucial steps; anticipate, identify and manage. These three steps will help you psychologically prepare for any emergency. It is all about getting in the right mindset.

Anticipate

Accept the fact that you are going to be a little stressed and anxious during and following an emergency. It is a natural human response. Although these are natural reactions, they are not always healthy or helpful. You need to be prepared to tame the urge to panic and run screaming into the wind.

Identify

Learn the physical responses to the feelings we mentioned above. Recognize the symptoms that will continue to lead to more thoughts of panic and anxiousness.

Manage

Once you know what is happening with your mind and body, it is time to regain control. Try a few deep-breathing exercises and positive self-talk to tame your anxiety. You want to be calm, cool and collected so you can make good decisions.

Now that you are aware of the three main components of a survival strategy, let's break it down into a step-by-step process.

Step 1 Anticipate:

There are numerous disasters that come with plenty of warning. You may live in an area where there are sirens indicating tornadoes or hear news reports of an impending hurricane or snow storm.

The warnings are typically accompanied by a list of instructions about what to do to prepare for the storm i.e. buying batteries for your flashlights, non-perishable food and so on.

Unfortunately, some of these dire warnings include horror stories with images of past devastation to really drive home the point. This can wreak havoc on a person's psychological state. These warnings can leave a person feeling more scared than they were in the beginning along with anxious and nervous.

Anticipating your responses will help you settle your nerves and give you an advantage. Expect the situation to be extremely tense and stressful. How are you under pressure? If you are cool as a cucumber, you are golden, if you freak out and have a panic attack, you need to start thinking about how you are going to control your responses to the stress.

Plan on how you will overcome your typical responses to stress so that you CAN make those life-changing decisions on the fly without letting your emotional response to the stress rule your choices.

Step 2 Identify:

Don't ignore the feelings and thoughts you experience when you hear those warning sirens or hear about a disaster headed your way. You need to recognize the "tells" and be ready to deal with them.

People generally have the same physical responses to extreme nerves.

- Rapid heart rate
- Difficulty breathing
- Upset stomach
- Shaking
- Sweating
- Tense muscles

The physical discomfort of these responses will trigger a string of thoughts that will pull you into the panic mode. You may start telling yourself;

- I can't do this.
- I won't make it.
- I don't know what to do.
- I am panicking.

From those thoughts, the physical symptoms are heightened and more thoughts enter your brain. It is a rather vicious cycle.

Learn to identify the thoughts that are causing the physical responses. You have to get a grip on your wayward thoughts.

- Identify the negative self-talk that is stressing you out.
- Quickly determine whether the thoughts in your head are helping or hurting the situation. The phrases above are not helpful and should be ignored.
- Don't be too hard on yourself. Those thoughts are typical, but not helpful. Identify and prepare to manage them.

Step 3 Manage:

There are two ways to manage those frightful thoughts that are sending you into a panic.

1- Adopt positive self-talk strategies.

2- Practice deep-breathing to control the onset of physical symptoms.

Controlling the fear with breathing and self-talk

It may sound incredibly simple, and it is, but it is also incredibly effective. Check out these tips to help use the breath you take to manage your stress while silently repeating positive phrases.

- Take a slow breath in through the nose, hold it for about three seconds and exhale through the mouth. Do this several times.
- While doing your deep breathing, in your head, say things like; I'm okay, I can do this, I am not panicking.
- Remind yourself that being calm and focusing on what you have to do is more important than the negative thoughts flitting through your brain.
- Remind yourself of what you have done to prepare for disaster. Fall back on any training or knowledge you have.
- It's okay to have the feelings that are common in a stressful situation, but it isn't okay to let them rule you. Accept your human nature and move on.

Helping Others Cope

You are going to need help with the survival business and need everyone around you to be ready and able. That means they too are going to need to manage their psychological responses. You can help.

- Don't judge others who are going through the emotional and psychical responses of a stressful situation. Offer

124

your support.

- Encourage others to use the deep breathing techniques.
- Ask them to tell you what they are feeling so you can help them work through those feelings.
- Give them the positive encouragement they need to
- hear and tell them to keep saying it to themselves and others.
- Keep everybody busy. You don't want them sitting and dwelling on all the negatives.
- Assign them a task and empower them to get it done.

Dealing with the Fallout

There are some emotions and feelings that you are going to be faced with in an emergency situation that has you fighting to survive.

Cold and Heat

One of your biggest concerns in a survival situation is the ability to stay warm or to stay cool.

Humans are typically 98.6 degrees. If they warm up a few degrees or drop a few degrees in temperature, things can get extremely difficult. Humans were designed to be at that one particular temperature and even the smallest deviation can cause serious problems.

You can increase your chances of surviving the cold by finding shelter, eating, staying busy and staying dry. It is crucial you are always prepared for the weather, especially when traveling. Dress appropriately for the climate you are in and headed towards just in case disaster strikes.

When the body becomes cold, you begin to feel numb. When the body becomes overheated, it becomes weak. Heat is something the body can slowly adjust to. It can take several days, but eventually, your heart rate, breathing and sweating are all adjusted to match a hot climate. You are also more prone to dehydration in the heat.

Heat poses more problems than just being uncomfortable in general. In the desert or in plain areas, it is hot during the day and cold at night. These temperature fluctuations can wreak havoc on your mind and body. Knowing how and where to find shelter will help you avoid the temperature extremes.

The glaring sun can also cause serious problems. The eyes and skin will suffer when exposed to direct sun for any length of time. It is important to protect the eyes with sunglasses or improvised eye wear and to wear clothing that protects the skin. It doesn't matter if you already have a tan; the sun exposure will still cause burning, dehydration and pain.

Hot, dry winds are another source of discomfort you can expect to deal with. This is especially true if you are in a desert area and sand is everywhere. Cover your face with a cloth, leaving only enough room to see out of.

Yet another issue you will face with blowing winds in snow or sandy situations is disorientation from being unable to see. This creates a horrifying situation for anybody caught in the storm. Feeling lost and unable to identify landmarks that will guide them can be extremely stressful. Being prepared to hunker down in such situations is the best option.

Along with extreme disorientation, desert situations may present mirages. These are images that are not truly there, but the mind's eye sees them. It can lead to a person walking into a hole or off a steep incline because depth perception is completely off.

If you find yourself in a windy situation, it is important you keep your mouth closed—literally. Talking and breathing through the mouth will dry out the mucous membranes. This triggers a thirsty response that can trigger discomfort and stress as well as lead to rapid dehydration.

Pain/Injury

Pain is your body's way of telling you something isn't right. You have to listen to your body and the signals it sends. Although pain may be screaming at you, you must make an effort to ignore it and push on. If you were not in a survival situation, sure, you could sit down and spend some time babying the injury. If you have over-the-counter pain meds, pop a couple and keep going.

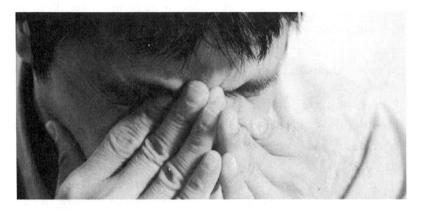

Pain itself isn't going to harm you, but it will make you uncomfortable. With adrenaline pumping through your system, you can push through the pain. People have managed to run miles on a broken ankle or climb rocks with a broken hand. It is all about using your brain to eliminate the pain. You CAN concentrate hard enough to minimize or completely dissolve the pain that is trying to slow you down.

Basically, acknowledge the pain and make up your mind to deal with it and it quickly becomes more tolerable. It is amazing how much a person set on surviving can cope with and overcome to reach their goal of living through whatever disaster has befallen them.

Dehydration

Dehydration is one of the most serious problems a survivor will face.

Although the human body can technically live 3 days without water, after the first few hours without water, the psychological impact of being thirsty will be extreme.

You can overcome this by remaining calm and focused on surviving.

Thirst is a tricky thing. It tells you the body is thirsty, but it doesn't say HOW thirsty. Do you

need a little water to wet your whistle or do you need a lot to keep your organs functioning?

You can still become dehydrated even if you are regularly drinking small amounts of water.

You can help combat the feeling of being thirsty and ultimately dehydrated by drinking as much water as you can when it is readily available. It is also important to drink water while you are eating.

If you are scared, sick or working hard, you will need more water to stay properly hydrated. Even mild dehydration can cause symptoms that will hamper your ability to survive.

Performance decreases and irrational behavior increases the more the body becomes dehydrated.

Fortunately, dehydration is a fairly easy fix—drink water. You can reverse the effects by getting fluids in your body as quickly as possible.

Hunger

Feeling hungry is not pleasant. Surprisingly, many survivors are unaware of the nourishment available to them in their surroundings. They don't see a cheeseburger and assume there is nothing to eat. Fasting for short periods of time may not be pleasant, but it is not going to result in anything terrible. You will live and you will not experience any real negative consequences.

Fortunately, with all there is to do in survival i.e. escaping, running and evasion, your hunger is completely forgotten about. In fact, plenty of folks who have survived disaster go for days without eating anything and they pull through without having any long-lasting problems. Of course, you want to avoid starvation by making sure you do have some food or a way to procure food.

If you don't eat, you are going to experience some psychological symptoms. You can stave off the hunger pains by drinking water, but you are still likely to experience depression and be a bit cranky. Relationships will be tried when one or more people are starving. Natural instinct will keep you on the hunt for food, which is great, as long as you are making good, sound choices in the hunt.

Food aversion in general may lead to starvation. Imagine the only food available was grubs. You may feel that starving is better than eating the bugs. However, if you are in a group and others choose to eat the grubs, you may be more inclined to follow suit. It's all about getting rid of old prejudices and open your mind to trying new things.

It is imperative you learn to control your hunger and accept the more primitive offerings available in a survival situation.

Fatigue

Fatigue is going to wear you down when you are hungry, thirsty and on the run. The stress alone will make you tired. A survivor is going to have to be vigilant in combating the effects of being tired that will decrease efficiency and effectiveness. Fatigue may be just one of many factors weighing down a survivor.

In the height of an emergency, a survivor will likely be forced to put forth considerable energy and exertion to do what must be done.

You have to determine how much you can carry, how far you can walk and how hard you can work and be prepared to fall back on those emergency energy reserves you are likely carrying and unaware of.

Do not allow yourself to become completely exhausted. Exhaustion can cause psychological and physical problems. Yes, there are going to be times when you will have to work no matter if you are tired, but when possible, avoid complete exhaustion.

Rest is the only effective way to overcome exhaustion. You have to take a break otherwise you risk making the crash from the extreme exhaustion more severe. The more fatigued you are, the longer your recovery will be. Taking breaks and getting rest early on in the survival game will keep your muscles and your mind primed and ready to go.

Taking short breaks during extended periods of stress will improve your total efficiency. The regular rest periods will also keep up morale. You also won't have to worry about getting bored with some of the more tedious jobs when you can take a break during the work period.

If you are doing extremely strenuous work, plan on taking more rest breaks. This can be said for especially tedious or monotonous jobs as well. If you are doing a lot of thinking and planning, taking a break and getting a little exercise is what is needed.

Sometimes, breaks don't even have to include actually stopping working. Sometimes singing while working, chatting with a friend or even telling jokes can help relieve the tension and give the mental break that is needed.

When planning breaks, it is important to consider the impact on the actual survival. If you have to walk 30 miles in order to reach shelter, stopping and resting several times may not be the best idea. Survival needs must always be put first.

One of the best ways to make the workload manageable is by working SMARTER not HARDER. You don't have to run or speed walk if you have a long way to go. Slow and steady is smarter way. Balancing the pace and effort you are expending will help you work smarter and not harder. Find a rhythm and go with it without taxing yourself.

In order to reduce fatigue, it is essential to have the cooperation of the entire group and a strong leader who can lead and encourage others to stay focused on the tasks at hand without overdoing it.

Fatigue will start to show itself psychologically as well as physically. Subtle changes in mood will show up as the body starts to slow down.

Avoid even the slightest bit of fatigue by instituting regular rest breaks early on. Survival doesn't have an expiration date. Plan for the long term and do what you can in the beginning to maintain your stamina. Sometimes, people will ignore the signs of fatigue, even when they don't have to, and push through. They will push themselves too far. You and the rest of the group need to be able to help others see the benefit to rest periods and not reaching complete exhaustion.

Isolation

Isolation is one of the most difficult psychological aspects of survival that a person will have to learn to overcome. While we all appreciate a little time to ourselves now and again, complete isolation will be difficult. In today's world, we don't realize how good we have it with our family, friends, co-workers and military colleagues always around us.

Long periods of time on your own can start to wear you down. However, you can resist the depression associated with isolation, by making a real effort to resist the feelings of loneliness. Embrace the solitude and accept it for what it is.

Sleep Deprivation

Losing sleep and experiencing sleep deprivation will look a lot like fatigue. Sleep deprivation can cause the following symptoms.

- Irritable
- Emotional
- Weary
- Inefficient/nonproductive
- Some of the causes of sleep deprivation are as follows
- Sleeping at odd times i.e. during the day, early hours of the morning
- Not getting the requisite amount of sleep needed, 6 to 8 hours
- Sleeping in unfamiliar places

- Restlessness

Every person will respond differently to the above factors. Some people may be able to sleep through anything, while others will struggle to sleep at all. A person who is in good shape can go 5 days before feeling the effects of sleep deprivation.

You can overcome sleep deprivation by trying some of the following tactics.

- Top physical shape
- Good mental state
- Access to food and water
- Plenty of opportunities to rest
- Company-companions

The key is to get as much sleep as possible whenever you can. If you are in a situation where you have to stay awake, moving or exercise, eating and good old conversation can help keep you going. Little catnaps will also help keep you alert.

When you stop moving, the sleepiness will likely come in waves. You may feel fine one moment and then dead tired the next. The breaks in between alert and sleepy will get shorter, the longer the sleep deprivation continues. A person who doesn't get sleep and continues on the sleep deprivation path will eventually become reckless. The sleep deprivation will lead to careless decisions that could jeopardize their life.

Depression

Survival can throw you into a tailspin, straight into depression if you allow it.

It is by far one of the biggest psychological hurdles you will have to deal with in a disaster situation.

Some feelings that indicate depression are prolonged periods of:

- Grief
- Disappointment
- Loneliness
- Sadness

Fortunately, the depression is likely temporary and will not become a chronic issue. Some symptoms associated with depression are listed below.

- Fatigue
- Appetite loss
- Fear
- Guilt
- Lack of interest in anything
- A feeling of helplessness
- Physical pain
- Suicidal thoughts

Experts are convinced that a person who battles bouts of depression in today's world will be more prone to depression in a survival situation. Depression can be dangerous. It tends to ride the coattails of other feelings. If you are fatigued or sleep deprived for long periods of time, you may become depressed, which heightens the fatigue. It is a vicious cycle.

Depression is more common once a survivor has secured everything necessary for survival i.e. food, water, shelter and so on. Once the survivor is "done" working, they have too much time on their hands to dwell on all the bad stuff. One way to stay busy after all the hard work is done is to keep making improvements to what is already completed.

Low Self-Esteem

Your self-esteem comes from your own personal pride and self-respect. If you have been a captive for some time, you may begin to doubt yourself.

Captors take great joy in humiliating their captives, which will erode at your self-esteem.

Humiliation chips away at your feelings of worth and makes you feel disgraceful or dishonorable.

The key is to hold on to your pride with all you have.

Anything a captor does is not in your control. They can do a lot to you, but they CANNOT take your pride. Survivors who have been captured and held prisoner may feel embarrassed or ashamed, but it is crucial those feelings are not allowed to rule your thinking and destroy your self-esteem.

Fear

Fear can be deadly. Fear in a survival situation may be brought on by a survivor's insecurity about what is happening and their ability to handle it or the presence of enemy forces nearby. The fear itself may be for a valid reason or a completely imagined one. No matter what the case is, fear can lead to panic. Survivors must learn to identify the symptoms of fear and work hard to get it under control.

There are some people who fall back on their training when put into a fearful situation and they do just fine. Military personnel are prime examples. Those who realize they can manage a situation will get a healthy boost of confidence and will not experience as much fear as someone who has little confidence.

On the flip-side, there are some people who panic in the face of fear and become paralyzed. They can't move their body or mind and do nothing, which is

always going to end badly. The response to fear is going to depend on the person. You can't assume the big, burly guy is going to be the calm, cool, collected guy in a fearful situation.

Anybody who faces a life-threatening situation is going to know what fear is. Fear is a direct response to the recognition of a dangerous situation or an impending danger. Fear has a way of stirring up other feelings like depression, unease, worry and a feeling of being uncomfortable. Every person's response to fear may be different. There may be some mild unease to full blown panic.

People fear many things. The fears may have been taught to a person at an early age or learned through personal experiences. Some kids tend to naturally fear the dark, certain animals and noises and even other adults. Through these fears, certain behaviors arise.

If a fear is allowed to spin out of control and create a fantasy disaster. This can lead a person to make choices that are reckless and will only further endanger them. The key to overcoming fear is by deciding it isn't there. The feeling isn't valid. Tamp down the fear and control the body and mind to make the best decisions possible.

Accept the fear for what it is and learn to overcome it. Training is one way to do this. Getting proper training in dealing with emergency and survival situations can give you the confidence needed to ignore fear and its tendency to make you irrational. The body will kick into autopilot so to speak and fall back on the training you have gone through when that fear is triggered.

The following tips will help you overcome and manage fear.

- Build up your confidence. Get the training you need and stay on top of your skills.
- Be prepared to deal with anything. Yes, it can happen to you. Always be ready with the right gear and clothing.
- Get informed and always be on the lookout to learn more about survival in different environments.
- Stay busy and keep on top of your duties of finding food, water and shelter.
- Worship and focus on your religion. Faith gives you something to believe in.
- Cooperate with a team. There is strength in numbers. Practice good teamwork and you will be better for it.
- Be disciplined and ensure your entire group practices good discipline.
- Keep a positive survival attitude. You and your entire group need to stay positive and fight off the feelings of depression and sadness that will bring you down. Expect to be slightly uncomfortable and accept it. You can't waste time and energy worrying about little things.
- Practice what you preach. Be the example for the rest of the group. Stay calm and your group will.

Hold on to what you believe in and never compromise your morals and values. People have been known to live through horrible events by embracing a feeling of calm when they rely on what is most important to them whether that be faith, morals or honor. You can overcome fear with training, knowledge and working together.

Panic

Panic can make a person act irrationally. A person who is panicking may not have any control over their actions. Some people are more prone to panic than others. An emergency situation is a common cause of panic.

The panic is triggered by overwhelming fear. Calming the fear will reduce the panic. Bolstering a person's confidence and setting a calm tone can combat the panic.

Anxiety

Anxiety is a common response to a change in a living situation or a person's safety being threatened. Anxiety and fear look a lot a like.

However, anxiety is a more mild form of fear. The feelings are not as intense. A person may feel anxious and not even know the cause.

Anxiety is caused by the feeling that something isn't right or something is going to happen. Some people describe anxiety as getting butterflies in their stomach. Worry, depression and uneasiness are also common symptoms.

Someone who has anxiety may feel;

- Indecisive
- Fear
- Depression
- Resentment
- Helplessness

You can overcome anxiety by choosing not to dwell on the problem or situation. Keep your body and mind busy on tasks that will help your situation.

Resentment

You may experience a feeling of resentment towards somebody that you blame for your situation. The resentment harbors feelings of indignation and displeasure and may have been caused by a simple remark or an act. You may even resent somebody in your group if it appears they are doing better than you. You may resent a captor or a group that has inflicted the pain and suffering of survival upon you.

The key is to accepting that nothing ever goes according to plan. In a tense situation, there are sure to be some negative remarks or insults. Don't let them get to you. They are not hurting you or holding you back from doing what needs to be done to survive. Approach the situation with an ounce of humor and you can negate the feelings of resentment. A lack of self-confidence and extreme stress can play a role in the feeling of resentment as well.

Hate

Hate is a strong word and an even more powerful emotion. It can be a good thing or a bad thing.

Hate is something that is built up based on knowledge or perception of a given situation. It doesn't matter if the information is true or not; hate can still be fostered.

Hate can be triggered by a person, object or beliefs. Hate has been used as a crutch in the past for prisoners of war who fed on the vengeful feelings that hate spawns. However, hate can also blind a person and they will make irrational decisions based on their desire for revenge.

To cope with hate, dig deep and identify where the feeling is coming from. Identify the reasons and then determine what you can do about it. Sometimes, there is truly nothing to be done and acceptance is the only recourse. Never allow hate to control you and your decisions.

Boredom

Boredom may look like fatigue, but they are not the same. A person who is bored will have a general lack of interest in anything. The feeling is typically accompanied by depression, anxiety or stress.

The feeling is exacerbated when there is no relief in sight. Relieving boredom must involve breaking up the uniformity and repetition of the situation.

By varying duties and methods to complete the duties, you can relieve boredom. Taking breaks is another option. Changing up the way things are done or switching jobs with somebody else in the group can help relieve boredom. Allowing the brain to think of new jobs or more efficient ways of getting something done will also give a person a goal to work towards, which will keep boredom at bay.

Impatience

Impatience may seem like a personal problem, but it can quickly manifest and actually become a serious problem that jeopardizes your life in a survival situation. If you are on the run and grow impatient with the waiting and hiding, you could end up exposing yourself and getting captured.

Survivors must accept that the situation may result in pain, discomfort and irritation without making a fuss. Endurance is the key. Getting impatient and acting out on that impatience can be dangerous. Take a few deep breaths and remain calm.

Anger

Anger can be brought on by anything that you perceive as being wrong. It makes you unhappy. The anger may be the result of being unable to fulfill a desire. If the anger is allowed to fester, it can turn into outright hostility.

Whoever or whatever triggered the anger will be the subject of your ire and you will have an urge to hurt or destroy the culprit.

Anger can lead to impulsive behavior, which is dangerous in a survival situation where every move must be calculated. You can get rid of the anger by taking a walk, yelling, exercise or get away from the source. You must control your anger in order to stay in control of your decision making and avoid acting irrationally.

Hopelessness

Hopelessness is that horrible feeling you get when you assume living or completing a task is impossible. The feeling may stem from the assumption that things are only going to get worse and everything is completely out of your control. Hopelessness may creep when you get the idea things are never going to get better. Some other situations that you may experience a sense of hopelessness in are;

- Getting home alive
- Recovering from an injury
- Seeing a loved one again
- Ability to cope with the mental and physical strain of the situation

Hopelessness may be worse in situations where you are exposed to the elements and physical and mental exhaustion take hold. Hopelessness can be deadly. There are cases of people dying in captivity for no real cause except the fact they actually willed themselves to die because of sheer hopelessness.

People who give up assume there is no hope. They gave up and decided it was fate to die. People who are headed down this path will generally withdraw from a group, become lethargic, lie down and ultimately die.

You can treat hopelessness by getting plenty of rest, seeking comfort from others and participating in activities that will help boost morale. Another option is to get mad or make somebody mad who is feeling hopelessness. Anger will fuel the person on in their desire to get revenge. It gives them something to live for. Staying positive will combat hopelessness and is the most effective remedy.

There are some cases where the situation cannot be resolved to the survivor's liking. This is when it is time to compromise. Accepting a compromise can help alleviate the feeling of total hopelessness in the situation. Taking any little concession will give you hope.

Imagine if you were starving. You may compromise your previous prejudices and eat bugs or a snake. You may resort to stealing. It is all about survival and doing what is necessary to reach that goal.

Loneliness can cripple you if you let it. One trick many people have used to overcome the feeling is to become more self-sufficient and adapt new routines while surrounding themselves with protective persons.

This is a skill that needs to be worked on before a survival situation pops up. Learning and developing the skills necessary to survival is important.

The more confidence and competence a person develops, the more self-sufficient they will become.

When a person who is self- sufficient is thrust into a survival situation, they are prepared to plan and stay active to combat those feelings of loneliness that may crop up.

Dependence

Getting captured and becoming a prisoners is the prime environment for feeling dependent.

Captors will intentionally foster this feeling by making the captive dependent on them for food, shelter and medical care.

The captor will make sure the captive is aware of their own need to take care of themselves. The captor will work hard to create a dependent relationship and then exploit it. It is important the captive recognizes this tactic and take steps to counter it.

Finding a way to take care of even one need is one way for a captive to take back even the smallest bit of control over their life. Holding on to anything they can will help them persevere.

Finding the Will to Survive

The will to survive means you are willing to do what it takes to survive despite the odds going against you. Participating in survival training, reading books and your own effort to hone your skills will play a huge role in your survival. There are plenty of cases that sheer will and determination were the deciding factors in keeping somebody alive. A person with all the training and knowledge in the world will perish if they do not have the will to survive.

Some examples of rare, but true cases of survival include one person eating their belt for nourishment. Another case involved eating human flesh and another boiled water in a boot and drank it as a nourishing broth. The will to survive will drive you to do things you normally wouldn't even consider.

Yet another shocking story of survival involves a man lost in the desert for 8 days without food or water. He lost about 25 percent of his total body weight. His blood had become so thick due to a lack of water, that when he cut himself during his travels, he couldn't bleed. It wasn't until he was rescued and re-hydrated that he began to bleed. His journey is a prime example of will and determination to survive no matter what obstacles were presented.

Sadly, the lack of the will to survive can have the exact opposite effect. Another story that didn't have such a happy ending involves a pilot who had to crash-land his plane. He did so and landed in one piece. He spotted shelter and a shoreline that would have provided food and water in the distance. He started out, but then turned back. He climbed back into his plane, enjoyed a cigar and then shot himself in the head. Within 24 hours, a rescue team arrived. He could have survived.

While it is difficult to try and reason away his decision, it is really just as difficult to think of reasons why somebody would eat a belt. It is all about the will to survive or the desire to give up.

Overcoming the Stress of Survival

We have talked a lot about using your mind to overcome the trials of survival. When things are at their worst, you have the power to overcome and conquer anything with sheer will. This will is what gives you the strength to keep going. Will is what mends the gap between the crisis and coping periods.

The Crisis Period

This is when realization about the situation dawns. There is no denying what is happening and it is time to figure out what to do. Shock is a common response as the mind struggles to acknowledge and accept what is happening. For those who have trained and prepared, the shock wears off quickly and springing into action is second nature.

For those who didn't prepare, shock will be intense. The body's response to the anxiety will leave the person with jumbled up thoughts and an inability to take action. A person in shock will need direction. A natural leader in the group will step up and start to direct those that are struggling. If the shock is allowed to rule, especially in a group setting, disorganization and chaos will quickly ensue. Judgment will be impaired and bad decisions will be made.

If a person is all alone when disaster strikes, it is important they gain control of the situation quickly and not let the shock rule. Prioritizing needs and taking action will need to happen sooner rather than later.

The Coping Period

This is when reality starts to sink in. This is when survivors make the decision to survive and fight. Coping with the pain, discomfort and poor situation will be necessary. Accepting the situation for what it is and doing what is necessary to keep going will all happen during this period. Coping requires a person to be in control and not allow panic and hopelessness to rule. Making good decisions that are conducive to survival depend on the control of the psychological responses to disaster.

Hunger won't kill you those first few days, but a lack of control of one's psychological responses will. Someone who survives will have to practice patience and be willing to stay put if that is what is necessary. When you are tired, hungry and uncomfortable, your first reaction may be to remedy those problems, but in doing so, you could be risking your life. This is why control of the emotional responses is crucial.

Positive Attitude

Keeping a positive attitude and committing oneself to surviving is essential. Nearly anything is possible if you set your mind to it, including survival. Often times, love for someone or something is what drives a person to that attitude of survival at all costs.

Love and hate are two very strong emotions that can give a person a great deal of strength and power they may not have known they had. The lack of the will to survive is just as powerful. A person who is unwilling to do what needs to be done or unwilling to take control of their emotions will suffer.

Possessing the will to survive is the key to surviving a situation. First and foremost, a person must fight the urge to panic and run. Taking a seat, getting control of your emotions and plotting out a course of action is necessary. Once a plan has been formulated, it is time to take action. Some people may be used to others doing this for them. In a survival situation, that is NOT an option.

Survivors have to be willing to control their emotions and formulate plans on their own.

Choosing to do nothing and taking a wait and see approach could be devastating. It is a choice that could cost somebody their life. Flexibility will be necessary, even if you have come up with an awesome plan. Expect the unexpected.

Tolerance

Coping with being uncomfortable, hungry or in pain will be a part of survival. You will be forced to tolerate situations like being in the dark or crawling through mud. Environments that you are not comfortable will have to be tolerated in order to meet your goal of surviving.

Optimism

You can't give up and you cannot assume something can't be done. You have to remain optimistic and look for the silver lining in every situation. So you have to walk an extra five miles, look at the bright side, you are going to get to sleep in a shelter instead of sleeping out in the open. Pray or meditate if it helps you hold on to that positive outlook that will keep you going and give you the strength you will desperately need.

Conclusion

Many survivalists and preppers get caught up in the mindset that the food, water and ammunition they store will be what gets them through. Survival is a mental game.

You have to learn how to cope with everything that will be thrown at you and learn to control your emotional response to those things.

Keeping a healthy state of mind is more important that finding water. You have to remain in control and be able to make sound decisions that will help you and not hamper your survival.

Losing focus and losing control of your emotions could be devastating.

While you are prepping for a disaster, don't forget to practice psychological preparedness as well.

Learn how to meditate and learn those deep-breathing exercises that will help you control your physical response to the emotional stress that is sure to come your way.

You will panic if you do not recognize the symptoms of panic or anxiousness. You must be able to recognize the symptoms so you can quickly get them under control before they lead you to make hasty decisions that are based on fear and not logic.

Keeping a positive attitude and embracing a will to survive will carry you through a lot.

Focus on anticipating, identifying and managing the various emotions that will arise on an almost hourly basis as you go through the aftermath of disaster.

Don't let prepping consume you. You have just learned what anxiousness and fear looks like. Take time to enjoy your life today.

Your "normal" life will likely give you plenty of opportunities to practice the skills we just covered. The next time you hit your thumb with a hammer, see what you can do to manage the pain. Practice your mental muscles as well as your physical muscles.

.